ROMANS
The Gospel Of Grace

William MacDonald

Original text material by William MacDonald
Developed as a correspondence course by
Emmaus Correspondence School,
which is an extension ministry of
Emmaus Bible College
founded in 1941.

ISBN 0-940293-32-3

34567890/4321

INSTRUCTIONS TO STUDENTS

We designed this material to serve as a guided self-study correspondence course for your personal enrichment. You may use it that way or as a guide for a group Bible study. There are several different groups of people who take these courses. Please follow the instructions for your group.

INMATES IN CORRECTIONAL INSTITUTIONS

This book will contain one of the following ways for sending us your answers. Please pick the one that applies to you.

A. When exams are bound in the book or are separate from the book and there is no separate answer sheet, remove the exams from the book after you take all the exams. Send them to the people who sent the course to you.

B. When you receive a separate one-page answer sheet, write your answers on the sheet. Please return it to the people who sent you the course.

C. When the exam questions are separate from the book, and you have a one-page answer sheet, send only the one-page answer sheet to those who sent you the course.

INDIVIDUALS USING THE COURSES FOR THEIR OWN STUDY

A. Cost

When you purchased this course, the price did not include grading. We would encourage you to take advantage of the personal help you will receive by taking it as a correspondence course.

Send $2.00, along with the name of the course, and your name and address, to the address on the back cover. (If you received the course from an Emmaus representative, send the money and information to them.) You will receive an educational package, including a single page answer sheet, that will enroll you in the Emmaus Correspondence School.

B. Taking the Exams

As you study the material, you will come to exams on various sections of the book. Take each exam as it comes up recording your answers. When you have taken all the exams, transfer your answers to the single page answer sheet and return it for grading.

You will receive a credit certificate if your average grade is 70% or higher. If your average grade is less than 70%, you will receive a completion card.

C. Other Services

Emmaus offers about 60 books of Bible study presenting Salvation, New Testament Book Studies, and Topical Studies. These books are available to you from the office in Dubuque (see address on back cover). If you would like the convenience of service closer to home, let us know. We will send you the name of an Emmaus Associate Instructor in your area.

ABOUT ROMANS THE GOSPEL OF GRACE

Paul's missionary strategy was ever to concentrate on the big cities - Jerusalem, Antioch, Ephesus, Athens, Corinth. Plant a strong church in a big city and the rural areas can be evangelized from there. And what bigger city, what more important city, what more influential city was there in all the world than Rome? Paul had a passion to go to Rome, to evangelize the city, encourage the saints, enlarge the Church. He made it eventually - in chains. But, in the meantime, if he couldn't go to Rome, he could write. And so he did. The result of course was the epistle to Romans, Paul's doctrinal masterpiece and one of the most important books in the whole Bible.

Some of the material in the following lessons has been drawn from that very excellent book, "Christ's Vicar," written by the author's late friend, Mr. H. P. Barker. May these studies enrich and deepen the spiritual life of each student.

HOW TO STUDY

Begin by asking God to open your heart to receive the truths He would teach you from His Word. Read the lesson through at least twice, once to get the general drift of its contents and then again, slowly, looking up all Scripture references and examining all footnotes.

BIBLE VERSION

You may use any version of the Bible for general study. If you choose to take this as a correspondence course, however, please restrict yourself to either the Authorized (King James) Version (1611), or the New American Standard Version (1960), when answering exam questions. These are widely used versions. There are so many versions today that your instructor cannot possible check them all in evaluating your work.

THOUGHT AND RESEARCH QUESTIONS

Some exams contain questions designed to make you do original Bible study. You may use your Bible to answer these questions. They are clearly marked.

WHAT DO YOU SAY? QUESTIONS

Questions headed in this way are optional and no point value is assigned to them. You may freely state your own opinions in answer to such questions. Your candid answers will help your instructor get to know you better as an individual. They will also help us evaluate the general effectiveness of this course.

HOW YOUR PAPERS ARE GRADED

Any incorrectly answered questions will be marked by your instructor. You will be referred back to the place in the Bible or the textbook where the correct answer is to be found.

ABBREVIATIONS

AV - Authorized Version
RV - English Revised Version (1881)
ASV - American Standard Version (1901)
RSV - Revised Standard Version
TEV - Today's English Version
JND - The Holy Scriptures, A New Translation from the Original Languages, J. N. Darby

TABLE OF CONTENTS

Chapter One

Paul and His Plans

Romans 1:1-17

One of the easiest ways to understand this epistle is to think of it as a series of questions and answers. As the Apostle Paul wrote the letter, he was undoubtedly aware of difficulties that would arise in the minds of some, and of serious objections which would be raised by others. He therefore seems to mention these problems one by one; then he proceeds to answer them in a way that shows the book to be truly inspired of God. Someone has said that this epistle shows how God meets every attitude that the mind of man takes in relation to Himself and His truth.

We will think of the epistle as containing eleven main questions. If the student learns these questions, and the answers to them, he will at least have a working knowledge of the Epistle to the Romans. The questions are as follows:

I.   What is the subject of the epistle?
II. What is the Gospel?
III. Why do men need the Gospel?
IV. According to the Gospel, how can sinners be justified by a Holy God?
V.   Does the Gospel agree with the teaching of the Old Testament Scriptures?
VI. What are the benefits of the Gospel in a person's life?
VII. Does the teaching of the Gospel (salvation by faith alone) encourage or even permit sinful living?
VIII. Does the Gospel tell Christians to keep the law in order to lead a holy life?

1

IX. How, then, is the Christian enabled to live a holy life?
X. Does the Gospel, proclaiming salvation for Gentiles as well as Jews, mean that God has broken His promises to His earthly people, the Jews?
XI. How should Christians show by their everyday behavior that they have been justified?

In the course of these lessons, it will be necessary to use a few unfamiliar words such as righteousness and justification. However, these words will be explained as clearly as possible when they first appear, and it is important that the student should thoroughly understand their meaning.

We proceed now to our study of Romans by considering the questions in order.

WHAT IS THE SUBJECT OF ROMANS?

The theme of this letter is the Gospel. Paul introduces it almost immediately. After identifying himself as the writer, he tells us that, by a divine summons, he has been sent forth to preach the Gospel (v. 1). As we shall see, he mentions the Gospel three other times in this first chapter—in verses 9, 15 and 16.

WHAT IS THE GOSPEL? (1:1-17)

First of all, we might answer this question by referring to the dictionary. There we would learn that the word itself means *good news*. But Paul tells us at least six other important facts about the Gospel in this section.

1. Some Facts About It

It is the Gospel of God (v. 1). This means that God is the author of the good news. It was not made up by man.

The Gospel was promised by the prophets of the Old Testament Scriptures (v. 2). This remark might have been made especially for the benefit of Jewish people who believed the Old Testament, but who resented the Gospel as a new and false teaching. If these Jews would only turn to such passages as Deuteronomy 18:15 or Isaiah 7:14, they would find the Gospel promised very clearly.

The Gospel is good news concerning God's Son, the Lord Jesus Christ (v. 3). In fact, the Gospel is all about Him, this wonderful Person who is descended from David as far as His humanity is concerned, but who is demonstrated to be the eternal Son of God by His power to raise the dead (v. 4). He is both God and Man.

The Gospel is God's power unto salvation (v. 16). It is the instrument He uses for saving every man who believes on Christ.

The Gospel is for all men, for the Gentiles as well as the Jews (v. 16). This is a very important point. The Jews, to whom Paul often preached, hated to hear this. Frequently, therefore, in this letter, Paul has to contend that the good news is for all, and he proves it from the Scriptures.

The Gospel is the good news that men are saved by faith alone (v. 17). Here we come to the heart of the Gospel message. God saves men on the principle of believing and not of doing.

2.   It Demands Righteousness

In verse 17, we find the first occurrence of the word "righteousness" in the epistle. We shall, therefore, pause to consider its meaning. Actually the word is used in several different ways in the New Testament, but we shall consider only three.

First of all, it is used to describe that characteristic of God by which He always does what is right, just and proper. When we say that God is righteous, we mean that there is no unfairness, dishonesty, or wrong in Him. Here in verse 17, we learn that the righteousness of God is revealed in the Gospel. In other words, the Gospel tells how God can save ungodly sinners and still be just in doing so.

Then, secondly, the righteousness of God is used to describe

3

the standard of perfection which God demands of His creatures (Romans 10:3). Since He Himself is righteous, He requires absolute righteousness from those who would dwell with Him in heaven. As we shall see, man is unable to achieve this righteousness by his own efforts.

Finally, the righteousness of God refers to the perfect standing which God provides for those who believe on His Son, the Lord Jesus Christ (II Corinthians 5:21). Thus, those who are not in themselves righteous are treated as if they were righteous because God sees them in all the perfection of Christ.

Now, then, in the opening seventeen verses of his epistle, Paul has introduced his subject, and has stated very briefly some of the principal points which he will explain in greater detail as he proceeds.

REVIEW
Paraphrase of Romans 1:1-17

Chapter 1

1) This is a letter from Paul, a slave of Jesus Christ, who was chosen to be a special messenger for the purpose of proclaiming good news from God. **2)** This good news was promised by God through the prophets of the Old Testament. **3)** It is concerned with His Son, Jesus Christ our Lord. He was born of the lineage of David, as far as His humanity is concerned, **4)** but He is also proclaimed by the Holy Spirit to be the Almighty Son of God. The proof that He is the Son of God is found in His power to raise the dead.

5) It is from Him that I have received the undeserved ability and the authority to go forth to all nations on behalf of His Name, calling on them to obey the Christian faith. **6)** You are among those to whom I have been sent; you are called to belong to Jesus Christ.

7) This letter is addressed to all the Christians living in Rome, that is, to all God's beloved ones, those who are called saints. I wish you grace and peace from God our Father and from the Lord Jesus Christ.

8) First of all, I should like to say that I thank my God through Jesus Christ for all of you, because your faith in Christ is so outstanding that it is spoken of throughout the world.

9) In fact, God is my witness, whom I serve wholeheartedly in the Gospel

4

of His Son, that I am so grateful for your faith that I pray for you unceasingly. **10)** I pray that in some way and at some time soon, I may be permitted by God to visit you. **11)** For I am anxious to see you, and to be of some spiritual help to you so that you will be strengthened as Christians. **12)** In that way, I shall be helped by your faith and you will be helped by mine.

13) I also want you to know, my brethren, that I have often planned to visit you, but have been prevented until now. You see, I desired that my ministry should have beneficial effects among you as well as among other Gentile people. **14)** For I have a sacred obligation to men of all cultures, both Greeks and barbarians, and to men of all degrees of intelligence, both wise and unwise.

15) Thus I stand ready and anxious to preach the Gospel to you in Rome.

16) It was not through shame of my message that I delayed coming to you until now, for I am not ashamed of the Gospel, even in Rome, for it is the power which God uses to save everyone who believes on Him. This power of God unto salvation was first made known to the Jews, and then to the Greeks and other Gentile people.

17) I am not ashamed of my message because the Gospel reveals to us the righteousness of God, that is, it tells us how God can justify ungodly sinners who receive His Son by faith, and how God can still be right in doing so. God's righteousness is revealed on the principle of faith from first to last. Those who believe on Him are declared to be righteous. This was taught in the Old Testament by the prophet Habakkuk when he said, "The righteous person shall obtain life by exercising faith." But it is the Gospel that tells us how this is possible.

GROUP DISCUSSION QUESTIONS
Chapter 1 — Paul and His Plans

1. What is the meaning of the word "Gospel"? How is the word "Gospel" related to Romans 1:1-6?

2. Why is it important for us to have Paul's attitude in verse 16? How can we demonstrate this attitude in our own lives?

3. Look up the word "righteous" in the dictionary. How can we be righteous when we are all sinners?

4. Look at verse 5 and at verse 17. What can we learn from these verses about the results of putting our faith in Jesus Christ?

Chapter Two

The Sin Question

Romans 1:18—3:20

In the previous lesson we discussed the question, "What is the Gospel?" We discovered that it originates with God; it was promised in the Old Testament; it is centered in the Lord Jesus; it is a powerful force for bringing all who believe into a right standing before God. In this lesson we are going to ask another question—

WHY DO MEN NEED THE GOSPEL?

The answer, in brief, is that all men are ungodly sinners and therefore exposed to the awful wrath of God. We are told in verse 18 that "the wrath of God is revealed from heaven against all ungodliness, and unrighteousness of men, who hold the truth in unrighteousness." Thus, apart from the Gospel, mankind is condemned and in imminent danger of hell.

1. The Heathen (1:18-32)

Now, one of man's favorite arguments, when told that he is lost, is this, "What about the heathen who has never heard the Name of Christ?" This age-old question is answered in verses 19-32.

Every man may know that there is a God by the works of

creation (vv. 19, 20). God's eternal power and deity are exhibited by the sun, the moon, the stars, the human body, animal and vegetable life, and in scores of other ways. He expects man to recognize Him as Maker, to glorify Him as God, and to be thankful for His creation and preservation and every other blessing.

The trouble is, however, that man has rejected the witness of creation to God (vv. 21, 22). For this reason, he is without excuse. Instead of worshipping the only true God, he has made idols resembling human beings, birds, animals, and snakes. These have become his gods (v. 23).

Of course, such dead idols cannot inspire men to live holy lives. Rather, men worship these false gods so that they can indulge in all kinds of sin without fear of punishment. They refuse the true God and substitute carved images so that they can live as they please. Accordingly, "God gave them up to uncleanness" (v. 24); man went deeper and deeper into heathen darkness and immorality until he indulged in the vile sexual behavior described in verses 26 and 27. From then on, his life became filled with the terrible sins of verses 29-31, and he took added pleasure in encouraging others to do likewise.

2. The Jews (2:1—3:8)

Having demonstrated that the heathen or Gentile is lost, Paul now takes up the case of the Jews (2:1—3:8).[1] Surely this privileged people to whom God gave the law is not under condemnation! Yes, the Jew, too, is lost in sin.

While criticizing their Gentile neighbors, the Jews were committing the same sins themselves (2:1). Because God did not punish them immediately, they thought they were getting away with it (v. 3). Actually, God was simply giving them time to repent (v. 4), but they kept on sinning and thus increasing their guilt at the day of judgment (v. 5).

God's judgment would surely come, however. These verses

---

[1] Many scholars believe that Paul does not address the Jew directly until verse 17.

(2-16) give the principles on which God's judgment is based. If a man could show that by patient continuance in well-doing he sought for glory and honor and immortality, he would be awarded eternal life (vv. 7-10). However, this passage does not teach that any can ever be saved in this way. On the contrary, ch. 3:19. 20 conclusively prove that no one will ever be saved by good works.

God's judgment would be strictly impartial, whether of the Jews or Gentiles (v. 11). Those to whom the law was given would be judged according to the law (v. 12). The Gentiles, to whom no law was given, would be judged by the voice of their own conscience, which told them what was right and wrong (vv. 14, 15).

The Jews were proud of their many privileges as God's earthly people (vv. 17-20), but they did not practice what they preached (vv. 21-23), and so brought reproach on the Name of God (v. 24). They should realize that religious rites, such as circumcision,[1] are worthless unless a person's life agrees with his profession (vv. 25-29).

Does the fact that the Jew is lost mean that there was no advantage to being a Jew (3:1)? No, it does not mean that. There were many advantages—chiefly this—the Word of God was committed to this nation (v. 2). And God will still keep His promises to Israel, despite that nation's unfaithfulness, but He will not overlook their sin (vv. 3-8).

3. The Inevitable Conclusion (3:9-20)

What is the conclusion then? Simply this, that all men, Jew and Gentile, are sinners. The Old Testament teaches clearly that sin has affected the whole human race (vv. 10-12). It also teaches that sin has affected every part of man—his throat, tongue, lips, mouth, feet and eyes (vv. 13-18). The law condemns the Jews who were under it, and, in so doing, condemns everyone. Verse 19 declares that, in God's sight, the Jews are really a sample of the whole human race. God tested the sample under the law and found it

---

[1]Circumcision is a ceremony instituted by God in Genesis 17 as a sign of His covenant with Abraham. It was to be practiced on all male members of the family, and was expressive of death to the flesh. Israelites commonly referred to Gentiles as "the uncircumcised."

evil. Therefore, He pronounced the whole race sinful on the basis of the sample. The law has exposed the guilt of all mankind, and so it is obvious that no one can be justified by keeping its commandments.

REVIEW
Paraphrase of Romans 1:18—3:20

Chapter 1

18) Another reason why I am not ashamed of the Gospel is because mankind is doomed without it. The Scriptures show that God's anger is directed from heaven against all men who are ungodly, and who fail to do what they know to be right.

19) Man is not left in ignorance as to the existence of God. There are certain things about God that can be known by all men. God has revealed these things to them. **20)** For, ever since the time of creation, two invisible attributes of God are obvious to man whenever he looks on the work of God. These attributes are His eternal power and deity.

Thus all men are without excuse, **21)** because, although they knew these things about God, they neither worshipped Him as God nor were thankful to Him. Instead, they formed unworthy ideas about God, and because they rejected the knowledge that was given to them, their mental powers were decreased. **22)** They thought that they were exceedingly clever, but they proved themselves to be fools **23)** when they tried to depict the excellency of the incorruptible God by idolatrous images representing corruptible men, birds, animals and snakes.

24) Because of this, God abandoned man to a state of moral impurity. By yielding to the evil impulses of their own hearts, they violated the chastity of their own bodies among themselves. **25)** This is what happened to those who exchanged the truth of the one true God for the lie of idolatry, and who worshipped and served the thing created rather than the Creator Himself—the One who alone is worthy of everlasting adoration.

26) Secondly, God abandoned the human race to degraded passions. Women used their natural functions in a way that was contrary to nature. **27)** Men refused their normal instincts with regard to women, and rather turned to other men in flaming passion. They did things which were vile, and in return, they received a fitting reward in their own bodies.

28) Finally, because men refused the knowledge of God, He abandoned them to a depraved mind so that they committed acts unsuited to them as men. **29)** They became filled with all kinds of unrighteousness, fornication, wickedness, covetousness and malice. They became full of envy, murder, strife, deceit and bitter enmity. They became gossipers, **30)** slanderers, haters of God, insulting, proud, boasters and wicked schemers. They became disobedient to their parents, **31)** without discernment, fidelity or love, unyielding and merciless.

32) These men know the verdict of God that the ones committing such sins are worthy of death. Yet they not only persist in doing them themselves, but they heartily encourage others who do them.

Chapter 2

1) In view of this sweeping condemnation of all mankind, no man can be excused for condemning another, because when he does so, he condemns himself. For the one who condemns another is guilty of doing the very same things. Therefore, he cannot be a true judge.

2) But we know that God's judgment is true in the case of men who commit these things.

3) Thus no man should think that he can judge others for doing the same things as he does, and still escape the judgment of God. **4)** Of course, God's judgment is not always immediate, and so men often belittle it by thinking lightly of the vastness of God's kindness and patience and endurance. They do not realize that during this delay God is seeking to lead them to repent of their sins.

5) In the meantime, because of the hardness and impenitence of his heart, man continues to become more and more guilty, until the day when God's wrath will be poured out, and when His righteous judgments will be made known. **6)** At that time, God will judge each one according to what he has done: **7)** God will award eternal life to those who, by their patient continuance in well doing, show that they are seeking for glory and honor and immortality.

8) On the other hand, those who are unrepentant and refuse to obey the truth, but instead obey unrighteousness,—those will receive indignation and wrath.

9) Trouble and sorrow will be the portion of every evildoer, of the Jew first because he is first in privilege, and also of the Greek and other Gentiles.

10) Glory, honor and peace will be the portion of those who have been delivered from evil works and have been characterized by good works, of the Jews first and then the Greeks.

11) For God does not make exceptions because of a man's nationality or because of human distinctions.

12) Neither can any man excuse himself on the ground that he is not accountable to obey the law. Those who did not hear about the law will be judged apart from the law. Those to whom the law was given will be judged by the law. **13)** For there is no merit in simply hearing the law. Rather it is obedience that counts with God.

14) Although the law was not given to the Gentiles, they have an inner knowledge of right and wrong. In this sense, they are living under a law. **15)** Even if they do not have the law, their own consciences provide a law for them. Their actions show the result of the law. God has put a consciousness of what is right and wrong in their hearts. Their conscience confirms this in their lives, and their thoughts continually either condemn or defend their actions.

16) Thus, as we have seen, the Gentiles who have lived in violation of that which they know to be right will be judged in a coming day. God will expose the secrets of men by His appointed Judge, Jesus Christ, according to the Gospel message I bring to you.

17) But does this excuse the Jew from the condemnation of God? Here you are, a Jew by name. You think that you are safe because you have the law. You boast about God as if He were exclusively yours. **18)** You think you are the only one who has had the revelation of His will. You think that, because you have been educated in the law, you have superior discernment. **19)** You confidently consider yourself a leader of the blind, a light for those who are in darkness, **20)** a corrector of the foolish, a teacher of beginners. You feel this way because, in the law, you have the outline of real knowledge and truth.

21) But let me ask you: As you teach others, why do you not take to heart your own lessons? You declare that a man should not steal. Do you not steal, thus breaking the commandment? **22)** You say a man should not commit adultery. Do you not commit adultery, thus breaking the commandment? You hate idols, but is it not true that you commit sacrilege yourself? **23)** You boast about the law, but is it not only lip service after all? Each time you break the law, are you not dishonoring God? **24)** Isaiah was right when he said that your inconsistent behavior causes God's Name to be blasphemed by the non-Jewish people.

25) You present-day Jews have the idea that no circumcised Jew goes to hell. But I want to tell you that circumcision is only of value when it is accompanied by obedience. If a circumcised Jew lives in disregard of God's law, then he might just as well be uncircumcised. **26)** On the other hand, if a non-

Jewish man, that is, one who is uncircumcised, lives in the will of God, is it not the same, as far as God is concerned, as if he were circumcised? **27)** And does not such a one put you to shame—you who with literal circumcision are law breakers? **28)** It is not the man who bears the outward appearance of a Jew who is a real Jew. Neither is true circumcision that which is outward in the flesh. **29)** A real Jew is one whose life agrees with his profession. And true circumcision lies not in the outward sign, but in the inward grace. True circumcision is spiritual, not literal. Men do not appreciate this inward grace, but God does.

Chapter 3

1) I can almost hear some Jew asking, "Well, what good is it to be a Jew if these things are so?" and "What is the value of circumcision?"

2) Well, for one thing, the Jews are highly privileged because it was to that nation that the Old Testament was entrusted. But the Jews have not believed.

3) A Jewish objector interrupts, "It is true that not all Jews have believed. But does that affect God's fidelity? Is He not bound to do for us all the things that He promised? Will we not all be saved because of God's promises to the nation? Can God break His Word?"

4) You should not even suggest that God could break His Word. No, indeed, we must steadfastly maintain the truthfulness of God, even at the cost of making every man a liar. David took this attitude when he said, "The complete truthfulness of every Word of Thine must be defended, and Thou must triumph every time Thou art called into question."

5) The self-righteous Jew continues with a typically human argument. "You imply that our unfaithfulness to our privilege serves to emphasize the fact that God is always right. If that is so, could God be fair in condemning us for our misdeeds? Our sins are bringing greater glory to God."

6) Your insinuation is preposterous! If God could be unfair, then He would not be qualified to judge the world, and we know He is going to do that. **7)** If your reasoning was right, I myself could argue as follows: If God's holiness is enhanced by contrast with my sinfulness, can He find fault with me as a sinner? **8)** Actually some people are falsely accusing me of teaching that we should do evil that good might be produced. I can only say that their doom is just.

9) What is the conclusion then? Are we Jews superior to the Gentiles? Not at all. I have already charged both Jews and Gentiles as being slaves to sin. This is conclusively proven in the Old Testament Scriptures. The following examples are cited:

10) "There is not one righteous person."

11) "There is no one who has a right understanding of God."
   "There is no one who seeks after God."

12) "All have gone astray from God."
   "All mankind has become corrupt."
   "There is not one who lives a good life, no, not one."

13) "Men's throats are like an opened tomb."
   "Their speech has been continually deceitful."
   "Their conversation flows from poisonous lips."

14) "Their mouths are full of cursing and hatred."

15) "Their feet are swift to carry them on missions of murder."

16) "They leave a trail of destruction and misery."

17) "They have never known how to secure peace."

18) and "They have no reverence for God."

19) Everyone knows that the message of the law from which I have just quoted is intended for those who are under the law. The failure of Israel under the law proves the failure of all men, since Israel is a sample of the race. Thus every mouth is shut, and all the world stands guilty before God. 20) No one can be saved by keeping the law. The law does not save. It shows men that they are sinners and therefore unable to keep the law.

GROUP DISCUSSION QUESTIONS
Chapter 2 — The Sin Question

1. How does nature show us the divine nature and power of God?

2. Why do you think some people prefer to worship gods that they have made with their own hands rather than their Creator? Why is this a foolish thing to do? What are the results which face those who give themselves to the sins described in Romans 1:24-32?

3. What is the "truth" that the Bible is warning us not to reject in Romans 2:8?

4. Discuss the results of Romans 2:11 for Jews (God's chosen people) and Gentiles. What nations could be compared to the Jews and Gentiles in the world around you?

5. Discuss the principle which is stated in Romans 2:13.

6. What is the meaning of circumcision in Genesis 17:9-11 as compared with Romans 2:29?

7. Can you find any comfort in Romans 3:10-20? Read on, there is hope for every sinner!

The Colosseum

Chapter Three

Salvation

Romans 3:21-31

Up to this point in our studies, we have seen that all men are sinners, and therefore subject to the wrath of God. A holy God must see that sins are punished, and the punishment He has decreed for sin is death. The great question then is this:

HOW CAN A HOLY GOD JUSTIFY SINNERS?

In the verses now before us, Paul sets forth the doctrine of *Justification* as the answer. This is a very important section, containing tremendous truths in condensed form. Before proceeding, however, we must examine the meaning of justification as set forth in the New Testament.

1. What Justification Is

Justification is the act by which God counts a sinner as absolutely fit for heaven the moment that sinner believes on the Lord Jesus Christ.

It does not mean that the believer becomes sinless or righteous in himself. Rather, God, as it were, covers him with a robe of righteousness. God now sees him as being in Christ and he is accepted, not because of who he is, but because of Christ's Person and work.

> "God sees my Savior, and then He sees me,
> In the Beloved, accepted and free."

Some have defined "justified"—just as if I'd never sinned. Others have expressed it—just as if I'd died. These meanings are all right as far as they go. However, they simply state that the penalty of sin has been paid by Christ. Justification goes beyond this and teaches that the believing sinner now has a perfect standing before God in Christ.

> "Near, so very near to God,
> I could not nearer be,
> For in the person of His Son
> I am as near as He."

As A. T. Pierson puts it, "God, in justifying sinners, actually calls them righteous when they are not—does not impute[1] sin where sin actually exists—and does impute righteousness where it does not exist."

But God does not compromise with sin or tolerate evil in the Christian. He first *reckons* men holy, and then proceeds to *make* them holy. This process, known as *sanctification,* will be completed when the believer is taken home to heaven.

2. How Justification Works

Now let us note carefully how Paul sets forth this thrilling truth. First, we learn in v. 21 that the righteousness of God has been manifested. This means that God has now revealed a way in which He imputes righteousness to sinners, and is still righteous in doing so. It is "without the law." Men are not justified by keeping the ten commandments, nor by human effort of any kind. It was

---

[1] Impute means to charge or credit to one's account. The New Testament speaks of Adam's sin being imputed or charged to every man, and of God's righteousness being imputed or credited to the account of every believer in Christ.

witnessed by the law and the prophets, that is, the Old Testament Scriptures agree with this teaching. It is "through faith in Jesus Christ" (v. 22). This is the means by which sinners are justified. It is "unto all, and upon all them that believe" (v. 22). There is no distinction between Jew and Gentile—all have sinned, and therefore all need the righteousness of God. It is offered to all, and imputed to all who believe (vv. 22, 23). Men are justified "freely by His grace" (v. 24). This not only means that men do not have to pay for salvation, but also that they do not deserve it. The only reason God bothers with man at all is because He is a loving, merciful, gracious God.

Justification is "through the redemption that is in Christ Jesus." This is the basis on which God can save man. He could not overlook sin or excuse it. The law demanded the death of the sinner. God must see that the demands of the law were met. So He sent His sinless Son to die as a substitute for ungodly men. Christ paid the penalty of the broken law for all who receive Him by faith. Christ has thus become a "propitiation" (v. 25). This means that, by the shedding of His precious blood, all the righteous demands of God have been met. God is satisfied with the work of His Son. Therefore, He can now show mercy to those receiving the Savior.

The Gospel further explains how God forgave the sins of the people in the Old Testament (v. 25). "The remission of sins that are past" refers to sins committed before Calvary. These were forgiven on the basis of the work of Christ which was still future. Old Testament believers looked forward to Calvary by faith, while today we look back to it. Thus, it is clearly shown how God can justify all who believe in Jesus, and still be just in doing so (v. 26). His righteousness demanded the death of the sinner, but His love desired the salvation of the lost. By sending His Son to die for men, He solved the problem in a satisfactory manner.

This plan of salvation eliminates all human boasting (v. 27). If men could be saved by doing something, then they might boast. But there is no merit attached to believing God. It is the reasonable thing to do.

The conclusion then is that man is justified by faith alone, and not by the deeds of the law (v. 28). This justification is for the Gentiles as well as the Jews (vv. 29, 30). The Gospel does not do away with the law (v. 31). The law of God demanded either perfect obedience or the death of the one who broke it. Since all men have broken the law, all are guilty of death. But, as we have seen, Christ died to meet the full requirements of the law for the sinner. Thus, when we preach salvation by faith, we uphold the law by insisting that its utmost demands have been fully met.

The glorious truth of justification has been beautifully expressed in a poem by Albert Midlane, entitled "The Perfect Righteousness of God."

"The perfect righteousness of God
    Is witnessed in the Savior's blood;
    'Tis in the cross of Christ we trace
    His righteousness, yet wondrous grace.

"God could not pass the sinner by,
    The law demands that he must die;
    But in the cross of Christ we see
    How God can save, yet righteous be.

"The sin alights on Jesus' head,
    'Tis in His blood sin's debt is paid;
    Stern Justice can demand no more,
    And Mercy can dispense her store.

"The sinner who believes is free,
    Can say, 'The Savior died for me';
    Can point to the atoning blood,
    And say, 'This made my peace with God.' "

REVIEW
Paraphrase of Romans 3:21-31

Chapter 3

21) But now God's plan for justifying sinners is made known—a plan quite distinct from the law, although attested by the Old Testament Scriptures. 22) God's justification is given to sinners when they put their faith in Jesus Christ. This justification is for all men, Jews and Gentiles, because there is no difference—23) all have sinned (in Adam) and continually fall short (in themselves) of God's requirement, which is absolute perfection. 24) Sinners can only be justified freely, by God's kindness through the redemptive work of Christ Jesus.

25) God ordained Christ to be His channel of mercy for those who by faith receive the benefit of His blood. In doing this, God revealed His plan of justification. He showed that He was right, after all, in His dealings with sins committed before Calvary. He merely let those sins pass for the time being. Those who believed on Him were saved on the basis of the work of Christ which was yet future. God was showing His patience during this time.

26) Now, in the death of Christ, God's righteousness is declared. God is just because He punished sin when Christ became the sin-bearer. Because of Christ's substitutionary work, God can now justify those who believe on Jesus.

27) Is there any room in this plan of salvation for man's boasting? No! If it were on the principle of works, there would be room for boasting. But when men are saved through faith alone, they have no reason to boast about it. 28) And that is how men are declared righteous—by faith, and not by works of the law at all.

29) If justification were by the law, then that would mean that only Jews could be justified, because the law was given solely to the Jews. Is God the God of the Jews exclusively? Is He not also the God of the Gentiles? Obviously He is! 30) There is only one God, and He justifies Jew and Gentile on the same principle—faith.

31) Do we then do away with the law by our constant emphasis on faith? Not at all! All the claims of the law were met by Christ's death. When a man receives Christ as his Substitute by faith, he stands before God as one who has paid the law's penalty. Thus the principle of faith insists that all the claims of the law must be met. We establish the law when we teach justification by faith.

GROUP DISCUSSION QUESTIONS
Chapter 3 — Salvation

1. Who can have God's righteousness and how can they get it?

2. Romans 3:12 tells us that we are all sinners. How can God's plan be to justify and redeem sinful men?

3. How did God provide justification for those who lived and died before Calvary?

4. Look up the words redemption and justification in a dictionary. Use those definitions to put Romans 3:24 into your own words.

The Temple of Jupiter by the Agean Sea

Justified By Faith

Romans 4

In our last lesson we learned what it means to be justified. This raises another question—

DOES THE GOSPEL AGREE WITH THE OLD TESTAMENT?

Paul has already stated twice that it does, but he is now going to prove it. In doing so, he uses the examples of two men—Abraham, who lived centuries before the law was given, and David, who lived many years afterwards.

1. The Example of Abraham (1-5)

How was Abraham justified? If it were by works, then he could boast before God. But this is impossible. No creature can ever boast before the Creator (v. 2). The Old Testament clearly tells how Abraham was saved (Genesis 15:6). He was reckoned[1] righteous by believing God (v. 3). Thus God justifies the ungodly, not by works, but by grace through faith (vv. 4, 5). Grace is the basis on which God gives salvation. Faith is the means by which man

---

[1] Reckon means to consider, regard or account.

receives it. Memorize these two verses in the translation which is appended to this lesson.

2. The Example of David (6-8)

Well, then, does David's experience agree with this? Yes, David speaks of the blessedness of the man whom God pronounces righteous, not by law-keeping, but simply by grace. He said, for instance, "Blessed are they whose iniquities are forgiven and whose sins are covered." This refers to a pardoned sinner, not an upright law-keeper (v. 7). He said also, "Blessed is the man to whom the Lord will not impute sin." Here, again, there is no mention of man's efforts. It is all God's grace (v. 8).

3. The Question of Circumcision (9-12)

But doesn't the Old Testament teach that circumcision was necessary for salvation? The answer is No. Abraham was justified before he was circumcised. He received circumcision later as an outward sign of the righteousness which he had obtained by faith in God. Thus, he became the father of all true believers.

4. The Question of the Law (13-25)

But isn't law-keeping connected in any way with justification? Not at all. Justification is by grace and not by law.

When God made His promise to Abraham that he would be heir of the world (through Christ), it was not on the basis of law. In other words, there were no conditions attached. It was not dependent on any works on Abraham's part. It was simply a promise from God that He would do it (v. 13).

Indeed, if the promise depended on keeping the law, then faith would be unnecessary, and the promise would be worthless because no one could meet the terms (v. 14).

All the law can do is condemn those who fail to keep it (v. 15). Thus, God has decreed that salvation should be by grace through

26

faith (v. 16). This is the only way the promise of eternal life might be *sure*. If good works were necessary, we could never be sure we had done enough, or had done the right kind. Also this is the only way the promise of eternal life might be sure *to all*. If man was required to *do* anything to be saved, there would always be some who could not meet the conditions. Belief on Christ is the only thing of which every person is capable without, at the same time, achieving any personal merit.

5. **More About Abraham (17-25)**

Abraham's case proves conclusively that justification is by faith (vv. 17-22). God promised Abraham that he would be the father of many nations. He told him that he would have descendants as numerous as the stars (vv. 17, 18). Humanly speaking, this was impossible. Abraham himself was about one hundred years old, and his wife was too old to bear children. Up until now, they did not have any family. Yet God had made the promise, and so Abraham dared to believe, knowing that God could perform the impossible.

> "Faith, mighty faith, the promise sees,
> And looks to God alone,
> Laughs at impossibilities,
> And cries, 'It shall be done.' "

"Therefore it was imputed to him for righteousness" (v. 22). Abraham's history was written as a lesson to us (vv. 23-25). He was not the only instance of where righteousness is imputed to a man by faith. God will do the same for us if our faith is in Him— the One who raised the Lord Jesus from the dead. He has promised eternal life to those who receive Christ by faith. Just as Christ was delivered to die on the cross because of our sins, so God raised Him from the dead in order that we might be justified through Him. His resurrection is a proof that God is satisfied with His work on Calvary.

Chapter 4

1) Let us consider an actual case to illustrate that justification is by faith and not by works. Take Abraham, our great ancestor, for instance. What was Abraham's experience with regard to the value of his own works?

2) If Abraham could have been justified by works, he would have had occasion of boasting of his own achievement. But no man can ever do this before God.

3) The Scriptures show that he was not justified by works. In Genesis we read, "Abraham believed God, and his faith was counted to him for righteousness."

4) Now if a man works for a reward, he earns it and can take personal pride in it. He deserves it. 5) But the man whom God sees as righteous is the man who does not try to work for his justification, but simply believes on God who justifies ungodly sinners.

6) David is another example of this same truth. He speaks of the happiness of the man who is declared righteous by God apart from any works of his own. 7) "Happy are they whose iniquities have been forgiven and whose sins have been covered. 8) Happy is the man to whom the Lord will not reckon sin."

9) Now is this happiness for the Jews only? Or is it for the uncircumcised nations also? Let us see. We have shown that Abraham was declared righteous by faith and not by works. 10) When did this happen? Was it after he had been circumcised, or before? Clearly, it was before. 11) Then after he was justified, he submitted to the rite of circumcision as an outward symbol of the righteousness which he had previously received by faith. Thus Abraham became the father of all who put their faith in God, including those who are not circumcised. 12) This experience is an assurance to the uncircumcised that they can be justified in the same way as he. He became the father of all who would afterwards be circumcised—not just those who had outward circumcision, but those who have the same faith as he had before he was circumcised.

13) God made a promise to Abraham and to his seed that he would be the heir of the world (through Christ). It was not made on the basis of law-keeping, but was a simple promise to be received by faith. 14) If blessing is contingent on keeping the law, then the principle of faith is excluded, and there is no hope of the promise being fulfilled. 15) A person cannot become

the inheritor of blessing by law-keeping because the law condemns. When men are not under law, but under grace, they are freed from the condemnation of the law.

16) Justification is by faith, so that it might be given undeservedly and unconditionally as far as human efforts are concerned. Because it is unconditional, it is sure to all people who have faith like Abraham, both Jews and Gentiles. In the sight of God, whom he believed, Abraham is thus the father of us all, **17)** as it is written, "I have made thee a father of many nations," for God makes the dead (Abraham and Sarah) to live, and speaks of persons not yet born (the seed) as if they were living.

18) Against all human probability, Abraham faithfully believed and he became the father of many nations, according to the Word of God, "Your seed will be great in number." **19)** Without being weakened in faith, Abraham took full note of the fact that he was about a hundred years old, and therefore too old according to natural laws to become a father. Likewise, he remembered that, humanly speaking, Sarah was too old to bear children. **20)** But he did not allow unbelief to make him stagger at God's promise. He became inwardly strengthened through faith, **21)** giving credit to God that He was fully able to do what He had promised. **22)** Because Abraham believed, God counted him righteous.

23) Now what applies to Abraham applies to us also. God caused this record to be written not only to show that Abraham was declared righteous, **24)** but also to show us that we, too, will be counted righteous if we believe on Him who raised up Jesus our Lord from the dead,—**25)** the same Jesus who was delivered up to be crucified on account of our trespasses, and raised again for our justification.

GROUP DISCUSSION QUESTIONS
Chapter 4 — Justified By Faith

1. What did Abraham do in Genesis 15:6 which allowed him to be saved? Is there any other way to be saved from the punishment we deserve for our sins?

2. Read Psalm 32:1-2. How did the Old Testament tell men they could be saved?

3. What was the purpose of circumcision? Do you think people used it as a "false god" in thinking that it would save them?

4. Does "keeping the rules" make a person righteous in God's eyes? Is there anything we can do that is good enough to cover our sins?

Chapter Five

Adam and Christ

Romans 5

Having explained the doctrine of justification by faith, Paul now turns his attention to the effects of this miracle in the believer's life. He is actually answering the very practical question, "Does it really work?"

WHAT ARE THE PRACTICAL BENEFITS OF THE GOSPEL?

In the verses that follow, he piles proof upon proof that the blessings of justification are wonderfully real.

It is to be noted that all these blessings flow to the believer through the Lord Jesus Christ. He is the Mediator between God and man, and all God's gifts are received through Him.

1. The Fruits of Justification (1-11)

Paul gives us six fruits of justification.

We have peace with God through our Lord Jesus Christ (v. 1). Formerly, we were at enmity with God. We fought against Him. We did not want Him to rule over us. But now the warfare has ended. We have surrendered unconditionally. A state of peace exists.

We have access by faith into this grace wherein we stand (v. 2).

31

The "grace wherein we stand" is the wonderful place of favor into which we have been brought by the Savior.

We rejoice in hope of the glory of God (v. 2). It is a joy to look forward to the time when God's glory will be seen by a wondering universe. All Christians share this hope.

We glory in tribulation (v. 3). We could not rejoice in trials when we were unsaved, but now we realize that only in this way can God produce certain graces in our lives, such as patience, experience, and hope.

We have the unshakable confidence that our hope will never be disappointed (v. 5). Christ will see us safely home to heaven. How can we be so sure? Because the Holy Spirit fills our hearts with the following proofs of God's eternal love to us. It was when we were without strength and ungodly that Christ died for us (v. 6). Will He do less for us now that we belong to Him? Christ died for us, not when we were decent or even good, but when we were sinners. Now that we are justified, will He not save us from judgment (vv. 7-9)? When we were *enemies*, we were reconciled[1] to God. Surely now that we are His *friends*, He will preserve us (v. 10). We were reconciled to God by the *death* of His Son. Death speaks of weakness. If His seeming weakness and defeat were sufficiently powerful to reconcile us to God, how much more will the power of His endless *life* insure our complete and final salvation (v. 10).

We joy in God (v. 11). This is quite a change. Before our conversion, we had no pleasure in God at all. In fact, it was only when we could forget Him that we were happy. However, now that we have been reconciled to God through Christ, we enjoy Him as the One who is nearest and dearest to us. (Note: The word "atonement" in this verse should be translated "reconciliation.")

Thus the Apostle concludes his catalog of the results of the Savior's work for the believer. In the verses to follow, he is going to gather up the threads of the argument so far in the epistle.

---

[1] Reconcile means to remove causes of enmity or unfriendliness, or to settle differences and to bring together in harmony.

2. The Summing Up (12-21)

Two main subjects have occupied our attention up to this point, namely, CONDEMNATION and JUSTIFICATION. Adam brought the former on the human race, and the Lord Jesus provided the latter. Now notice how Paul compares and contrasts the two.

Sin and death entered the world through Adam (v. 12). Adam really acted as a representative of all mankind. This may be illustrated by a well-known fact in human government. When the ruler of a nation signs an official document, he signs it for all the people in the nation. He is acting for them. Thus, when Adam sinned, the results of his act affected the entire race. When he sinned, all sinned, and death came upon all (v. 12).

This is proved in an interesting way. During the period from Adam to Moses, men did not have a law from God. They did not disobey any written commandments of God. Yet people died during this time—including infants who never knew right from wrong. Why did they die? Because they sinned in Adam.

Adam is a figure or type of Christ (v. 14b). Just as he acted as a representative for his race, so the Lord Jesus came to act in behalf of a new race. But notice these striking contrasts (v. 15).

It is true that because of one sin of one man, many have died. But think how much greater God's grace is than man's sin. And not only God's grace, but the gift which flows out to many through the Lord Jesus (v. 15).

The effect of one man's sin was that all men were sentenced to condemnation. How much greater is the effect of God's gift. It is not only freedom from condemnation, but a perfect standing before God. And this is true in spite of not just one sin, but many sins (v. 16).

By the one sin of one man, death reigned as a cruel tyrant. But by the gracious gift of Christ, men themselves reign like kings, enjoying the life which the Savior gives them (v. 17).

Thus, as by the sin of one man all men were condemned, so by Christ's righteous life at the Cross, justification is provided for all (v. 18).

And, as by Adam's disobedience, many were made sinners, so by Christ's obedience in death, the many who trust Him will be declared righteous (v. 19).

God gave the law so the awfulness of sin might be seen in its true light. But God's grace at Calvary was seen to be greater than all man's sin.

By the work of the Lord Jesus, the tyranny of sin and death has been ended, and those who trust Him are better off than if Adam had never sinned (vv. 20, 21). As long as Adam remained innocent, he could look forward to a long life on earth. But he had no promise of becoming a child of God, an heir of God, and a joint-heir with Jesus Christ. He did not have the prospect of a home in heaven, or of being with Christ and like Him forever.

Through the work of Christ, the believer has all these blessings, and many more in addition. Thus, it will be seen that:

> "In Christ the sons of Adam boast
> More blessings than their father lost."

Perhaps this is a partial answer to the familiar question: Why did God allow sin to enter into the world? God has gained more glory and man has received more blessings through the sacrificial work of Christ than if there never had been any sins to be put away.

REVIEW
Paraphrase of Romans 5

Chapter 5

1) And now, because we have been justified by faith, we have peace with God through our Lord Jesus Christ. 2) In addition, through Christ we have come into a place of absolute favor with God, whereas formerly we were banned from His presence by our sins. And we rejoice in the prospect of one day being with Him and being glorified with Christ.

3) Not only do we have these blessings, but we are enabled to be joyful in the face of troubles, because it is only through troubles that we can develop

the Christian grace of patience. **4)** When we are patient, we have an indication of God's work in our lives. This assurance gives us hope that He will finish the work He has begun. **5)** Hope does not disappoint us. We have unquestioning confidence in God because He has given us His Holy Spirit, who fills us with evidences of God's love for us.

6) God's love is seen in the fact that when we were totally unable to help ourselves, Christ came, and at God's appointed time, He died for ungodly men. Think of it—He died for *ungodly* men! **7)** We ourselves would scarcely think of dying even for an honest man, one who met all his obligations and was accurate in his business dealings. In fact, it is only remotely possible that some would be willing to die for a truly kind and generous man. **8)** But God demonstrates His love for us by this amazing fact—while we were still *sinners,* Christ died for us.

9) Now, if Christ has gone to such cost to justify us when we were sinners —the cost of shedding His precious blood—will He not surely deliver us from His judgment now that we are believers? **10)** For if we were reconciled to God by the death of His Son when we were active enemies, is it not obvious that now, having been reconciled, we shall be kept safe by His risen life, a life that is devoted to the best interests of His people? **11)** And not only shall we be kept safe, but we shall be kept rejoicing in God, through our Lord Jesus Christ, who has reconciled us to God.

(Indeed, everything in the way of divine blessing comes to us through our Lord Jesus Christ. God has used this Man to bring blessing just as one man previously brought a curse.)

12) It was by one man that sin entered into the world, and death came as the penalty for sin. Thus the sentence of death was passed upon all men, because they all sinned in Adam, their representative. Death came upon all men, not just those who had deliberately sinned. This can be definitely proved.

13) Up until the time of the law of Moses, sin was in the world. But God does not charge sin to a person's account when there is no law. **14)** Yet people continued to die during this period from Adam to Moses. Death reigned over the human race. People died although they had never sinned in the way Adam did, that is, by deliberately disobeying the Word of God. Why did they die? Because they were made sinners by Adam's sin. Adam acted as the representative of the race.

In that sense, Adam was the type of the One who was to come, the Lord Jesus Christ. **15)** But there the similarity ends.

First, there is a mighty difference between the fall of Adam and the gracious gift of God. In the one case, the fall of one man brought death to many. In the other case, God's gracious gift of His Son, Jesus Christ, has flowed out in life to many.

16) The fall is the opposite of God's gift in another way. The one sin of Adam resulted in God's judgment, condemning all to death. But in the face of not one but many sins, God's gracious gift has brought justification, not condemnation.

17) By one offence, death reigned supreme through that act of one man. But there is a greater reign than this. Those who receive God's abundant favor and His gift of righteousness shall reign in eternal life because of the act of one, Jesus Christ.

18) By the offence of one man, the sentence of condemnation of death passed upon all men. But by the righteous act of One, the message of justification of life is declared to all men.

19) By the disobedience of one man, many were made sinners. In contrast, by the obedience of one Man, many shall be constituted righteous.

20) The law was given so that it might increase man's knowledge of the prevalence of sin. But where sin was seen to be great, grace was seen to be all the greater. **21)** So, just as sin came to reign by inflicting death on all men, grace comes to reign righteously by giving eternal life through Jesus Christ our Lord.

GROUP DISCUSSION QUESTIONS
Chapter 5 — Adam and Christ

1. What unusual principle does Romans 5:3 state? Read the next two verses and discuss how this can be true.

2. How did God show His love? How does this realization affect our lives?

3. How did God make possible the provision of an abundant life for those who accept His gift of righteousness?

4. Compare Titus 3:5-6 to Romans 5:20-21.

The Constantine Monument

Chapter Six

On to Victory

Romans 6

We have seen that we can be justified by faith alone and not by works. This truth raises a question in the minds of some.

DOES THE GOSPEL PERMIT SINFUL LIVING?

When the Gospel of grace is preached, people invariably make the following objection, "If all you have to do to be saved is believe on Christ, then you can go out and live as you please." In this chapter, we learn why this is impossible.

1. **Knowing (1-10)**

The first great fact we meet is that Christians are "dead to sin" (v. 2). What does this mean? Simply this. Our old nature has been crucified with Christ. God was not interested in patching up or improving our evil, corrupt nature. His only remedy for it was death. Now when the Savior died, He died as our representative. In God's estimation, when He died, we died. All that we were by nature was nailed to Calvary's cross. Likewise, when Christ was buried, we were buried. That removed us out of God's sight forever as sinful creatures. Our old "I" has been put in its proper place.

This is all pictured by baptism (vv. 3-7). When we go beneath the water, we witness that we, as children of Adam, deserved nothing but death. We agree with God that our old self, or "old man" was unfit to live. We confess that we died with Christ, and were buried with Him. Since Christ died to settle the whole question of sin once for all, we admit that we no longer have any right to traffic with sin. We are dead to sin, not in the sense that we are sinless, but in the sense that God sees us as those who have died, and therefore sin has no claim upon us.

But Christ rose from the dead, and since we are in Christ, God sees us as having risen also (vv. 8-10). However, we do not rise to live the same old kind of a life. We ourselves have been crucified with Christ. We rise as new creatures with the object that Christ may henceforth live His life in us.

Now these are divine facts. Whether you feel them to be true or not, God says that every justified person is dead unto sin, buried with Christ, risen with Him, and given a new life—His life. He wants you to KNOW that this is true of you as far as your position before Him is concerned. He wants you to accept it by faith.

2. Reckoning (11-12)

The next step is to "RECKON yourself to be dead unto sin, and alive unto God" (vv. 11, 12). It is already so as to your standing; now let it be so as to your practice. Behave as one who is dead to sin, self and the world, and alive to God. Do not let sin reign over you. Remember that you have died to its claims.

3. Yielding (13)

Finally, the Christian is to YIELD himself unto God (v. 13). Let God control you. Turn over the members of your body to Him daily, yes, continually. Then, instead of living your own life and doing the things you want to do, you will allow Him to live His life in you.

4. Under Grace, Not Law (14-23)

Sin does not have dominion over the believer because he is not under law but under grace (v. 14). This is an important point.

When a man is under law, sin has dominion over him. The law tells him what to do, but does not give him the power to do it. Moreover, when you tell a sinful man not to do a certain thing, he immediately wants to do it all the more.

The Christian is under grace. Whereas law says, "Live a holy life and you will be a Christian," grace says, "You are a Christian by God's free gift; now live a holy life out of love for Him." Men will do out of love what they would never do by compulsion or from fear of punishment.

The fact that the Christian is not under law does not mean that he will want to live in sin. He has been given a new nature which hates sin. He is indwelt by the Holy Spirit of God who encourages and enables him to live a holy life. He remembers what his sins cost the Savior. He knows that he is the servant of whomever he obeys. He used to obey sin, but now he is ashamed of that kind of a life (vv. 16-21).

Therefore, the great desire in the life of the child of God is to yield himself as a servant of God so that the life of Christ might be reproduced in him (vv. 22-23).

REVIEW
Paraphrase of Romans 6

Chapter 6

1) What is our conclusion then? Shall we continue in sin that God's grace might be multiplied to us? Does this teaching of justification by faith give men the license to live as they please?

2) Perish the thought! When Christ died, we died with Him. We died to sin. Our connections with sin were severed. That being so, how can we go on living in sin?

3) Do you not know that those of us who were baptized unto Jesus Christ publicly identified ourselves with Him in all that He has done for us?

Included in His work for us was His death. Therefore we were baptized unto His death.

4) In the rite of baptism, we confess that we have been buried with Him in death, so that we might rise to live a new kind of a life, just as Christ was raised up from the dead by the power of God. **5)** For if we are associated with Him in this picture of His death (going down under the water), it follows that we are also associated with Him in this type of His resurrection (coming out of the water). **6)** For we must take into consideration the fact that our old self, our former manner of life, was crucified with Him, so that the body of sin might be rendered powerless, so that thereafter we should not be the slaves of sin. **7)** For he who has once died to sin now stands free from its claim. **8)** Since we died with Christ, we believe we shall have life with Him forever. **9)** We know that, since Christ was raised from the dead, He will never die again. Death has no claim on Him. **10)** For in that one death of His, he died unto sin. Now that He lives, He is living unto God.

11) In the same manner, you are to consider yourselves as dead unto sin, because you died with Christ, and alive unto God, because you rose with Christ. **12)** You are not, therefore, to allow sin to rule in that body of yours, which is still mortal, by yielding to its evil desires. **13)** And do not give over the control of the members of your body to be the tools of sin. But abandon yourself whole-heartedly to God as a testimony of what you really are—one who is alive from among the dead. And give God the use of your members that He may employ them as instruments of righteousness. Under the law, men did not have this glorious privilege. They were under the reign of sin. **14)** But sin shall not hold dominion over you, because you are not under law, but under grace.

15) What are we to conclude from this? Is it all right to commit acts of sin because we are not under law but under grace? Banish the thought! **16)** Do you not know that when you submit yourselves as servants by agreeing to obey a master, you become a servant of that master? That master may be sin, and service to sin leads to death. Or that master may be obedience, and service here leads to righteousness.

17) Now we thank God that, although you were once the slaves of sin, you have willingly accepted the teaching to which you have been delivered. **18)** You were freed from the yoke of sin and became bondslaves to the righteousness of God.

19) I am using this commonplace illustration of bondslaves because of the difficulty of otherwise explaining these truths to you.

Thus as you once abandoned your bodies as slaves of uncleanness and iniquity to practice iniquity, so now yield your bodies as slaves of righteousness with a view to growth in holiness.

20) When you were slaves of sin, you were free from God's righteousness. But what did you gain by it? **21)** Nothing but a list of things of which you are now ashamed. At the end of that path was nothing but death. **22)** But now that you are freed from the bondage of sin, and have become bondslaves of God, you have benefits in the way of holiness, and as its ultimate object, you have eternal life.

23) For the wages of sin is death, but the gift of God is eternal life in Jesus Christ our Lord.

GROUP DISCUSSION QUESTIONS
Chapter 6 — On to Victory

1. Why does Romans 6:6 call us "slaves to sin"?

2. What spiritual principles does Baptism illustrate (Romans 6:5-10)?

3. Do we have an excuse for our sins after we are saved since we are justified? Compare Romans 5:9 and 6:1,2,14.

4. Define wages and gifts. How do these words differ? Compare the results of sin and the gift that God offers us (Romans 6:23).

Chapter Seven

Bondage!

Romans 7

Paul has previously shown very clearly that man is not saved by keeping the law. But now another question arises.

MUST WE KEEP THE LAW ONCE WE ARE SAVED?

After a person is saved, is he not obliged to keep the law as a rule of life?

In the previous chapter, we learned that the Christian is not under law but under grace. The reason for this will now be made plain. In addition, the Apostle will demonstrate, from his own experience, the impossibility of a believer's achieving holiness by his own efforts.

1. Free From the Law (1-6)

The law has no jurisdiction over a person after he dies. This is illustrated by the law of marriage. This law binds man and wife together only as long as they are both alive. However, when one of them dies, the authority of the law is ended, and the living partner is free to marry again (vv. 1-3).

The child of God has become dead to the law through the body of Christ (v. 4). The Lord Jesus died to the law in the sense that

He paid its penalty for us. Since the believer is looked upon as having been crucified with Christ, he, too, has died to the law. Since all its demands have been met in the death of the Savior, the law has nothing more to say to the Christian.

This freedom from the law enables the believer to be married to Him who is raised from the dead (v. 4). The Lord Jesus, not the law, becomes the believer's rule of life. Marriage implies union. Union with Christ means sharing His life. It is far better to allow the life of Christ to be manifested in our mortal bodies than to seek to become holy by our own puny efforts.

Freedom from the law enables us to bring forth fruit unto God (v. 4). When the law forbids a certain thing, the human heart desires to do it all the more. Since the penalty for breaking the law is death, and since none of us has the power to keep the law, the only fruit we can bring forth under it is death (v. 5). Now that we are delivered from the law, we can serve the Lord with willing hearts, and not out of compulsion or fear (v. 6).

2. The Function of the Law (7-14)

Does this mean that the law itself is sinful? The Apostle emphasizes that it is not. Its very holiness reveals the greatness of man's sin. Paul would not have known, for instance, that evil thoughts, as well as wicked acts, are sinful except for the law, "Thou shalt not covet" (v. 7). But our sinful, corrupt nature uses the law to stir up all manner of evil desires within us, so that we long to do that which is forbidden. Thus, apart from the law, sin might be thought of as a sleeping thing. But when the law comes, sin wakens and becomes very active (vv. 8-11). The conclusion, then, is that the law is holy, just and good, showing sin in all its wickedness. But the human heart is depraved and wants to do what it is told not to do (vv. 12-14).

3. Trying Too Hard (15-25)

Attempts to lead a holy life by one's own efforts lead to

46

disappointment and despair. Paul cites his own experience in this connection (vv. 15-24).

He knew what he ought to do, but he could not do it. The things that he hated—those are the things he did. He acknowledged that the law was good, but his old nature was hopelessly powerless to obey it. The more he tried to do what was right, the more he seemed to fail. Finally, he came to the end of himself and was forced to confess defeat, "O wretched man that I am! Who shall deliver me from the body of this death?" (v. 24).

It was then, and not until then, that Paul realized that the secret of holiness was not to be found in himself, but in the Lord Jesus Christ. "I thank God through Jesus Christ our Lord" was his shout of triumph. It was only as the Lord was allowed to live His life in Paul that any measure of deliverance from indwelling sin was obtained (v. 25).

REVIEW
Paraphrase of Romans 7

Chapter 7

1) Do you not know, brethren—you who are familiar with the law—that a law only has claim on a person during his lifetime? **2)** For example, a married woman is bound by the marriage law to her husband as long as he is alive. When he dies, she is free from that law. **3)** Thus, if she marries another man while her husband is still living, she shall be known as an adulteress. If, on the other hand, her husband is dead, she is no longer bound by the marriage law, and does not commit adultery when she marries another man.

4) Now, brethren, consider your own relationship to the law in the same light. You were formerly married to the law. When Christ died, you died with Him. Therefore, you became dead as far as the law is concerned by the death of Christ. And you died to the law, not so that you would be free from all restraint, but so that you could be married to the One who rose from the dead, and thus bring forth fruit for God. This is something you could not do as long as you were under the law.

5) For when we were in the flesh, the sinful passions which were aroused by the restraints of the law were active in our bodies, yielding a harvest for death.

6) But now our status is that we have been delivered from the law, inasmuch as we have died to that bondage in which we were held, and now we have become God's slaves with a new attitude of willingness, and not with a reluctant attitude of trying to observe the letter of the law.

7) Do we conclude from this that the law is in itself sinful? Not at all! The law is definitely useful. It was only by the law that I became conscious of sin. For instance, I would not have recognized lust as sin unless the law said, "Thou shalt not lust."

8) But although the law is useful, yet by prohibiting certain actions, it arouses the desire to do these very things. Sin thus takes advantage of the commandment, which is good, and uses it to bring out in me all kinds of evil desires. For, in the absence of the law, sin was inactive.

9) To illustrate: Before I knew the law, I lived in a state of blissful ignorance of my own depravity. But when the law came into my life, sin became very real to me, and I became miserable. **10)** Thus the commandment which pointed to life actually, in its operation, condemned me to death. **11)** Sin used something which was good, that is, the commandment, to make me sin more. Thus it tricked me, and made me completely miserable.

12) The law itself is holy, and each commandment is holy, fair, and beneficial.

13) Is it possible then that anything so good might be the cause of sin and death in my life? No indeed! But sin is the cause. The law was given so that sin might appear as such, that it might become exceedingly sinful. But sin uses the commandment, which is good, to make me helpless, corrupt, miserable.

14) I know that the law is holy, but I am corrupt, subject to the influence of a sinful nature which I cannot resist in my own strength. **15)** My actions do not agree with what I know to be right. I fail to do the things that I approve, but I invariably do the very things which I disapprove. **16)** And when I do these things which I know are wrong, I do not prove that the law is evil, but rather that I am evil and the law is good. **17)** The very fact that I approve the law shows that it is no longer my real self which is disobedient, but it is the sinful nature that dwells in me. **18)** For I know that in me, that is, in my human nature, dwells no good thing. **19)** The good things that I want to do are not carried out. But the evil that I do not want to do—those are the very things I do. **20)** Since my actions do not agree with my desires, I realize that there are two conflicting forces within me.

21) Thus I find a principle at work, that when I want to do good, I do evil. **22)** For I delight in the law of God as far as my real self is concerned—that is, the law has the joyful approval of my renewed mind.

23) But there is another power at work within me, in constant conflict with my mental knowledge of what is right, and making me an unwilling captive to the power of the sinful nature which indwells me.

24) What a miserable man I am! Who can give me deliverance from this sinful burden? Can the law do it? **25)** I thank God that deliverance comes through our Lord Jesus Christ.

Then, to revert to my conclusion, I serve the law of God with my renewed mind, but with the flesh I serve the law of sin.

GROUP DISCUSSION QUESTIONS
Chapter 7 — Bondage

1. How does the idea of following the principles of the law relate to what you read in Romans 7:5-6?

2. Is it valid to make a comparision between the innocence of a baby and a person who does not know the law?

3. How does Romans 7:7-14 show us that we are like young children who are tempted to do exactly what we are told *not* to do? Does this make the rules bad?

4. Can you see yourself as being like the Apostle Paul in Romans 7:15-25? How?

Freedom!

Romans 8

We have already learned that it is not by one's own strength that sin's passions are restrained. In this chapter, we are taught that it is by the Holy Spirit, who indwells every true believer. As we turn over our lives to Him and allow Him to take control, He will deliver us from the power of indwelling sin by occupying us with Christ and changing us into His likeness.

HOW THEN CAN I LIVE A HOLY LIFE?

A holy life is the result of the Holy Spirit having His way in the believer's life. The results of this are numerous and blessed.

First of all, there is a new freedom (v. 1). "There is . . . no condemnation to them which are in Christ Jesus." Whereas efforts at law-keeping produce only bondage, life in Christ is perfect freedom. (Note: Many early manuscripts of the Bible omit the last part of verse 1, namely, "who walk not after the flesh but after the Spirit.")

Then, there is a new law of life (v. 2). "The law of the Spirit of life in Christ Jesus" has superseded "the law of sin and death." This may be illustrated as follows: When you throw a stone into the air, it immediately returns to the earth. The law of gravity has taken effect. When you toss a living bird into the air, however, it flies off into the heavens.

A new law has taken effect—one that is greater than the law of gravity. It is the law of life. Thus, there is a principle in every Christian like the law of gravity, always seeking to drag him down into sin. But the indwelling Holy Spirit is able to free the believer from the law of sin and death.

Again, there is a new power (vv. 3, 4). The law could not produce righteousness because of the fallen condition of human nature. But Christ, by His death, condemned sin in human nature, and ended its power over His people. Now the Christian is able to fulfill the righteousness of the law by the power of the Holy Spirit.

There are new desires (v. 5). The Holy Spirit directs the saint's mind away from things that please the flesh, and seeks to occupy him with the things in which God is interested.

There are new results (v. 6). Life and peace become the believer's portion. This is true life—life that is worth living. It is Christ's life, reproduced in us.

There is a new attitude toward God (v. 7). Loving submission replaces enmity and rebellion.

There is a new sphere of life—in the Spirit rather than in the flesh (vv. 8, 9). A person living in the flesh caters to his own desires and comforts. He acts as if his body and his possessions were the only things that really count. A person living in the Spirit turns his life over to God so that the Holy Spirit may have His way without being hindered.

There is a new guarantee (v. 11). The Holy Spirit in the child of God is definite proof that his body will be raised from the dead, just as Christ's was.

There is a new allegiance (v. 12). We owe all our loyalty to the Spirit, not to the flesh. We owe nothing to the flesh.

There is a new duty (v. 13). We are to mortify the deeds of the body through the power of the Spirit. This means to say "No" to every thought or deed that is unworthy of the Lord Jesus.

There is a new guidance (v. 14). True Christians enjoy the enviable privilege of being led by the Spirit of God. Instead of aimless wandering, there is planned progress.

There is a new sense of intimacy with God (v. 15). It is the freedom of a son rather than the fear of a slave. We can look up into the face of

God by faith and call Him "My Father."

There are new relationships (vv. 16, 17). The Spirit teaches the Christian that he is a child of God, an heir of God, and a joint-heir with Christ. Since we are members of the divine family, it follows that we will share all the Father's riches with Christ.

There is a new privilege (vv. 17b, 18a, 20-23). It is to suffer with Christ. This might not seem like much of a privilege at first. But when you realize that the Lord Jesus shares every pain, it becomes a blessing.

There is a new hope (vv. 23, 24). It is the redemption of the body. God's work in us will not be complete until He has taken these frail bodies of ours and freed them forever from the power and presence of sin.

There is a new prospect (vv. 17b, 18b, 19). We are going to be glorified with Christ. The whole creation, including the animal kingdom, is waiting for the time when we will be displayed as the children of God (v. 19). At present, this is a groaning, sobbing world, but a better day is coming, and for that day we hope.

There is a new assistance (vv. 26, 27). The indwelling Spirit helps us in our prayers. He knows what God's will is for us; and therefore He helps us to pray for this.

There is a new confidence (vv. 28-30). God is on our side.

Finally, there is a new assurance (vv. 31-39). No one can be successfully against us. We are on the winning side. We are more than conquerors.

Verses 33 through 39 of this chapter have been much loved by Christians of all ages and in all countries. Those who take the time to memorize them will be well rewarded.

REVIEW
Paraphrase of Romans 8

Chapter 8

1) There is, therefore, now no condemnation to those who are in Christ Jesus. **2)** For the new law under which I live as a Christian, the sway of the life-giving Holy Spirit, has freed me from the law which provokes sin and condemns to death.

3) The law told me what to do, but it did not give me the power to do it. But what the law could not do because it has no power to remedy sinful human nature, God accomplished by sending His own Son in the likeness of a human being. As an offering for sin, His Son condemned sin in human nature, ending its claim and power over Christians. **4)** He did this so that the righteousness demanded by the law might be fulfilled by Christians—those whose behavior is governed by the Holy Spirit and not by the lusts of the flesh.

5) For those who are governed by the flesh live to fulfill the desires of the flesh, but those who are governed by the Holy Spirit give first place to the things of the Spirit. **6)** The former path leads to death; the latter to life and peace. **7)** For those who are carnal in their thinking are hostile to God—they are not obedient to His law, which demands holiness, neither do they have the power to be. **8)** Those who are ruled by their corrupt nature cannot find approval with God.

9) But if you are indwelt by God's Spirit, you are no longer under the sway of the flesh, but under the Spirit's power. If a man does not have the Spirit of Christ dwelling within, he does not belong to Christ.

10) But if Christ dwells within, even if the body is still subject to death because of sin, yet the spirit is living because the righteousness of God has been imputed. **11)** And if the Spirit of the One who raised Jesus from the dead dwells within you, then that same One shall impart life to your mortal bodies by His Spirit who now dwells within you.

12) Now then, brethren, we are not under any obligations to the flesh to follow its orders. **13)** Indeed, if you do obey the lusts of the flesh, you shall die. But if, by the power of the Spirit, you put to death the evil works of the body, you shall live. **14)** For those who are governed by the Spirit of God are the children of God. **15)** You have not received a spirit that makes you a slave to anxiety and fears, but you have received the Spirit which tells you of your adoption as a child of God. It is this Spirit which enables us to address God as our Father. **16)** The Spirit assures our own spirit that we are the children of God, **17)** and that because we are children, we are heirs; heirs of God and joint heirs with Christ. We are joint heirs with Christ, sharing His sufferings now, in preparation for sharing His glory later.

18) For I do not esteem the sufferings of the present time as worthy of consideration when I think of the coming glory that is to be our portion.

19) All creation is looking forward to this display of glory. For even the creatures of the world are anxiously awaiting the display of God's children in glory. **20)** The creature was subjected to the curse which came upon all creation through sin. This did not come upon the creature through its own choice, but it came from God, the same One who has implanted in the creature the hope of better things to come. 21) The creature shall indeed be delivered from the present bondage to corruption which spells decay and death for everything.

22) For it is obvious to us that the whole creation has been groaning and agonizing in pain up until the present time. 23) And this includes those of us who are Christians, who are possessors of the initial results of the Holy Spirit's work—even we ourselves are inwardly groaning, waiting for the public display of our adoption, the time when our bodies shall be redeemed from corruption. 24) The salvation of the body is a blessing for which we hope. This calls for waiting. You do not wait for that which is already present. For if a man sees something, why should he live in expectation of it? 25) But when we hope for something which is not yet seen, then we await it with patience.

26) Not only does this hope sustain us in our sufferings, but the Spirit helps us to bear our infirmities. For instance, we do not know how to pray intelligently, but the Spirit Himself prays for us through groans and sighs—prayers which cannot be put into words, but which are heard and answered. 27) And God, who is able to read the hearts, knows the Spirit is praying, because the Spirit prays for the Christians in a way that is in full agreement with the will of God.

28) Because the Spirit is thus interceding, we know that everything that happens in the life of one who loves God, who is called according to His purpose, is working toward the Christian's ultimate good.

29) For all those whom God foreknew as belonging to Him, were predestinated by Him to be made like His Son, holy and without blame, so that Christ might be the pre-eminent One among many brethren.

30) Those who were thus predestinated, God called to Himself. Those whom He called, He justified. And those whom He justified, He also glorified.

31) What is our conclusion from all of this? If God is on our side, can anyone be successfully against us? 32) God did not spare His own Son, but delivered Him to be crucified for us all. Now, having done this, is there anything else that He will not do for us?

33) Who will bring any charge against God's chosen people? No one can in view of the fact that it is God Himself who justifies us. 34) Who will condemn us? No one can in view of the fact that Christ died for us, yes, even rose again, is even now at the right hand of God, and makes intercession for us.

35) Who shall separate us from Christ's love? Shall tribulation or distress or persecution or hunger or destitution or danger or the executioner's sword? 36)—imminent dangers of which the Psalmist wrote when he said, "For Thy

sake we are dying daily. We are treated like sheep who are about to be slaughtered."

37) No one of these things can separate us from Christ's love. In all of them, we are more than conquerors through Christ who loved us.

38) For I am utterly confident that neither death, nor life, nor angels, nor principalities, nor powers, nor present events, nor future events, 39) nor height, nor depth, nor any other created thing shall be able to separate us from the love of God which comes to us through Jesus Christ our Lord.

GROUP DISCUSSION QUESTIONS
Chapter 8 — Freedom

1. The first verse of Romans 8 makes a statement and the rest of the chapter explains that statement and gives us the results of it. Find the six divisions in this chapter.

   A. Statement of a great truth.

   B. Explanation of what this means to each person.

   C. What we should do in response to this information and why we should do it.

   D. What results we can expect in the present and in the future.

   E. Why did God do all this for us.

   F. Rejoicing in His love.

The Forum

Chapter Nine

The Case of the Jew

Romans 9-11

During the Old Testament, God's dealings were primarily with the nation of Israel. That was His chosen people, and it was to that people He made many great and precious promises.

Now that the Gospel message is preached to Gentiles as well as Jews, it almost seems as if God has forgotten about these ancient promises.

HAS GOD BROKEN HIS PROMISES?

No! Paul here explains that Israel has been temporarily set aside by God because of unbelief. However, when the nation again turns to the Lord, it will be restored to a position of privilege and favor.

We will consider the subject under three main headings.

1. Israel's Rejection Was Justified (9:1-29)

The nation had been highly favored. They had been adopted as God's own people; they had the glory cloud which signified His presence on earth; they had the covenants, the law of Moses, the Temple service, the promises and the patriarchs. Finally, the Lord Jesus was descended from Israel. In spite of all this, Israel rejected the Messiah and so has been set aside by God (vv. 1-5).

59

This does not mean, however, that God had been unfaithful to His promise. His promises were never made to all Israel, but always to a chosen or elect portion (v. 6). For instance, Abraham had many children, but only the descendants of Isaac were God's choice. Thus, the mere fact of one's ancestry does not insure blessing. Then, Rebecca had twin sons, Jacob and Esau; but the line of promise was only through Jacob. God made this clear before the boys were born, thus indicating that good works had nothing to do with His decision.

It will be seen, then, that God is sovereign. He can show mercy to whomever He pleases (vv. 14-18). No one can accuse Him of unfairness when He does it (v. 14). He told Moses that He would do this (v. 15). It is not a matter of man's effort, but of God's mercy (v. 16). When Pharaoh had hardened his heart against God, the Lord used him as an object lesson by which to demonstrate His power (v. 17). (Note: Although the Bible teaches that God chooses men for blessing, it never teaches that He chooses some to be damned.)

No man can question God's actions (vv. 19-21). To do so puts man on equality with God. All men come from the same lump of sinful clay. If left alone, they would all perish. God is the Potter. He comes in to His house and shows mercy to some. Does He not have the right to do this? As Charles Erdman says, "God's sovereignty is never exercised in condemning men who ought to be saved, but rather it has resulted in the salvation of men who ought to be lost."

God only rejected Israel after much patient long-suffering (vv. 22-24). Moreover, the salvation of Gentiles and the rejection of all but a remnant of Israel was predicted in the Old Testament. The salvation of Gentiles is discussed in verses 25 and 26 and the rejection of all but a remnant of Israel is discussed in verses 27-29.

2. Israel's Rejection Is Due to Unbelief (9:30—10:21)

The Jews sought to obtain righteousness in their own way, that is, by trying to keep the law (9:30-33). In other words, they refused to submit to God's way of salvation, which is faith in Christ (10:1-4). Moreover, Israel should have known from the Old Testament that righteousness is by faith, not by law (10:5-11) because Moses taught the difference. Law tells man to *do,* but faith says there is nothing to do. Christ has already *done* the work. He has come down into the world, has died, has been buried, and has risen again. Now, all God requires is that we confess Jesus as Lord and believe that God has raised Him from the dead.

Israel should also have known from the Old Testament that righteousness by faith is for all, both Jew and Gentile (10:12-21). Many of the prophets foretold it. Isaiah proclaimed salvation for "whosoever believeth" (v. 11). Joel promised salvation for "whosoever" also (v. 13). Isaiah and David both spoke of the world-wide proclamation of the Gospel (vv. 15, 18). Moses and Isaiah both predicted the calling of the Gentiles (vv. 19, 20), while Isaiah foresaw the rejection of the message by Israel (v. 21).

3. Israel's Rejection Is Neither Complete Nor Final (11:1-36)

God did not reject the entire nation (vv. 1-6). The Apostle himself is a proof of this (v. 1). Also, a remnant has been preserved by grace, even as in the days of Elijah (vv. 2-5). However, God has caused blindness to come upon Israel (vv. 7-10). This is not physical blindness, of course, but inability to see clearly in spiritual matters. Note also that Israel's rejection does not mean that the nation will be cut off forever (vv. 11-16). Their rejection has resulted in salvation coming to the Gentiles (vv. 11, 12). Moreover, Gentile blessing is intended to provoke the Jewish nation to jealousy (v. 14).

If Israel's downfall has meant blessing to the world, its restoration will mean even greater blessing (vv. 15, 16). Gentiles, however, should beware of the same peril which caused Israel's rejection (vv. 17-25). They should not boast. The Jews, after all, are the channel of blessing. They were rejected because of their unbelief. In vv. 17-24, Paul uses the figure of an olive tree to illustrate his teaching. The natural olive branches are the nation of

61

Israel. The wild olive branches are the Gentiles. The olive tree itself is the line of privilege through the world's history. Unbelief, therefore, is just as much a peril to the Gentiles as it was to the Jews (vv. 21, 22). It would be a much less violent process for God to restore Israel than it was to bring the Gentile people into blessing (vv. 22-24). Israel's blindness is only temporary (v. 25). For Israel will yet be restored (vv. 26-32).

Paul's conclusion is that God's ways are wonderfully perfect (vv. 33-36). The student should pay special attention to these verses. They really teach the truth that "God is everything and man is nothing."

REVIEW
Paraphrase of Romans 9-11

Chapter 9

1) I speak the truth as a Christian; I do not lie; my conscience approves what I say by the witness of the Holy Spirit, **2)** that I have a great burden and continual sorrow in my heart when I think of Israel. **3)** For I could wish that I were accursed from Christ for the sake of my brethren, who are my relatives. **4)** They are Israelites. They were the ones whom God first designated as His sons. It was among them that the glory of the Lord was manifested. It was with them that God made various covenants. It was to them that the law was given. It was to them the service of the tabernacle and the temple was entrusted. It was to them that promises of the Messiah were given. **5)** The patriarchs belonged to that nation. And it was of that people that Christ was born as to His human nature—Christ who is God over all, blessed for ever. Amen.

6) The fact that the nation of Israel is no longer in favor with God, does not mean that God has broken the promises He made to Israel. For those who are born unto the nation of Israel are not necessarily true Israelites. **7)** Just because a man is descended from Abraham does not mean that he is a child of promise. It was Abraham's posterity through the line of Isaac who were called by God. **8)** In other words, it is not the children who are born in the natural way who are God's children, but those who are born in accordance with God's promise. **9)** For this is the text of the promise which God made to Abraham, "At this time will I reveal my supernatural power, and Sarah shall

62

have a son."

10) And this is not the only instance that proves the case that God is sovereign in electing. When Rebecca conceived, it was by one man, our own patriarch Isaac. **11)** Her twin sons were not yet born, therefore neither had done good or evil. Yet, in order that God's determination to choose by sovereign election might be carried out, not according to works but according to God's own method of calling, **12)** it was said to Rebecca, "The older son shall serve the younger." **13)** This agrees with the Scripture which says, "I have preferred Jacob, but I have regarded Esau with less favor."

14) What shall we say about this? Is God unfair in acting in this manner? Not at all! **15)** God clearly said to Moses, "I will show mercy to those of my own choosing and have compassion on those on whom I wish to have compassion."

16) So then, you see, the attainment of God's favor does not come from a man's desires or his efforts, but from God's mercy. **17)** For example, the Scripture says to Pharaoh, "I have raised you up to your present position for this purpose, namely, that I might show my power in my dealings with you, and that My Name might be published throughout the world." **18)** Thus, God shows mercy to whomever He wishes, and He hardens others when He desires to.

19) You will probably say to me, "If that is the case, why does God blame us for anything? Who of us can stop His purpose from being carried out?"

20) That is the wrong attitude. What right do you have to speak back to God? Can the creature say to the Creator, "You are responsible for my condition?" **21)** Does not the potter have the right to make two different types of vessels out of the same lump of clay, one vessel which he approves, and another which he rejects?

22) Therefore, who can object if God, desiring to show His wrath and to make His power known, yet at the same time, acted with much patience toward the objects of His wrath, those who were fit subjects for destruction? **23)** This He did so that He might make known the riches of His glory on some of these vessels, which He had previously chosen as vessels to manifest His glory. **24)** I am speaking now of those of us whom He has called, not only Jews, but Gentiles also.

25) It is just as Hosea said, "I will call them my people which were not my people, and will call her beloved, which was not beloved."

26) And in another place, he said, "And it shall come to pass that in the place where it was said unto them, Ye are not my people, there shall they be called the children of the living God."

Thus the blessings of God are not limited to those who are outwardly considered to be His people. In fact, only a small portion of His people, Israel, will enter into blessing.

27) Isaiah cried out concerning Israel, "Though the number of the children of Israel be as the sand of the sea, only a remnant shall be saved, for He will finish the work of judgment quickly and righteously; it will be a brief work of judgment on the earth."

29) And as Isaiah had said previously, "Except the Lord of hosts had left us a remnant, we would have been like Sodom, and been made like Gomorrha."

30) What do we conclude from this? We conclude that the Gentiles who did not even seek after justification have attained to that justification which is by faith.

31) But Israel which sought the way of justification has not found it. 32) Why? Because they did not seek it in God's way, that is, by faith, but rather by the works of the law. For they stumbled at that stumbling-stone 33) as it was prophesied, "Behold I lay in Zion a stumbling stone and a rock of offense. Whosoever believeth on Him shall not be confounded."

Chapter 10

1) Brethren, the desire and prayer of my heart to God for Israel is that they might be saved. 2) For I can honestly say about them that they have a real zeal for God, but unfortunately it is not based on correct knowledge.

3) For they are ignorant of the way in which God provides righteousness, and they are seeking to establish their own righteousness. Thus they have not bowed to God's method of justification. 4) They have sought righteousness by keeping the law, but what they do not realize is that the law was given to show men their need of Christ, so that those believing on Him would be justified.

5) Moses described the method of justification which is based on the law as follows: The man who does these things shall live by so doing.

6) But justification by faith expresses itself in this way. Do not suggest that salvation is impossible by asking, "Who shall go to heaven to bring Christ down?" 7) Or, "Who shall descend into the abyss to bring Christ up from the dead?" 8) How does it express itself? The answer is within you, in your mouth, in your heart. It is the message of faith which we preach 9) that if you shall confess with your mouth Jesus as Lord, and believe in your heart that God raised Him from the dead, you shall be saved. 10) For when man believes with his heart, he is justified, and then he confesses with his mouth that he is saved.

11) The Scripture says, *Whosoever* believes in Him shall not be disappointed **12)** for there is no difference between the Jew and the Greek. The same supreme Lord shows His great resources to all that call on Him. **13)** *Whosoever* calls on the Name of the Lord shall be saved.

14) But if the message is for all, how can men call on the Lord in whom they have not believed? Or how can they believe in Him if they have never heard of Him? Or how can they hear without a preacher? **15)** Or how can men preach unless they are sent to preach? There must be a preacher if all are to hear. Isaiah predicted this, saying, "How welcome is the coming of those who preach the Gospel of peace, and bring glad tidings of good things."

16) But they (Israel) have not all obeyed the Gospel. Just as Isaiah said, "Lord, how few of them have believed our announcement of the Messiah!"

17) Now then, faith comes by hearing, and hearing by the Word of God.

18) But I say, "Have they not heard?" Yes, indeed, "Their voice went throughout the earth, and their words to the uttermost parts of the world."

19) But I say, "Did not Israel know that they would be rejected and the Gentiles called?" They should have known because Moses said, first of all, "I will make you jealous by those who are not even a nation in My sight, and I will anger you by an idolatrous nation." **20)** Then Isaiah is very blunt when he says, "I was revealed to those who did not even seek Me. I was made manifest to those who did not want Me." **21)** But to Israel God says, "All day long I have extended My hands to a disobedient and rebellious people."

Chapter 11

1) I ask then, "Has God cast away all His people completely?" Not at all. I myself am proof that He has not. I am an Israelite, a descendant of Abraham, and born of the tribe of Benjamin. **2)** God has not rejected His true, spiritual people, that is, those whom He chose. Are you unfamiliar with what the Scripture says in speaking of Elijah, and in describing how he cried out to God against Israel, **3)** "Lord, they have killed Thy prophets, torn down Thine altars, and I am left alone." **4)** But what was God's answer to him? "I have kept for Myself seven thousand men who have not bowed the knee to Baal."

5) Thus, in the same way, there is at this present time a remnant of Israel which God has chosen by His grace. **6)** And since it is by grace He chose them, then works have nothing to do with their salvation. Otherwise, grace would no longer be free and apart from works. If they were chosen because of their good works, then grace could not be involved.

7) What is the conclusion then? The entire nation of Israel has not obtained the justification for which it sought; but the chosen portion of the nation has obtained it. The rest were judicially hardened just as it is written, **8)** "God has given them the spirit of deep sleep, eyes that do not see, and ears that do not hear up until this present day."

9) And David said, "Let their blessings become a snare, a trap, a cause of stumbling, and a retribution to them. **10)** Let their eyes be blinded that they may not see, and let them be bent over as in old age."

11) I ask then, "Is the purpose of Israel's stumbling that they might be forever cut off?" No, the purpose is rather that as a result of their fall, salvation might come to the Gentiles so as to provoke Israel to jealousy.

12) Now, if Israel's fall has meant blessing to the world, how much more will their recovery mean. If the loss of Israel's position means wealth for the Gentile, how much more will Israel's restoration mean?

13) For I preach to you Gentiles because I am the apostle of the Gentiles. I really fulfill my office in emphasizing these truths. **14)** I seek by every means to provoke those who are my kinsmen to jealousy, so that I might be used in the salvation of some of them.

15) For if the rejection of Israel has resulted in the Gentile world being brought nigh to God, what will the restoration of Israel be—it will be the same as a glorious resurrection for the entire world.

16) God has not forgotten that He consecrated the patriarchs to Himself. If these men, the first-fruits, were consecrated, so are the mass of their descendants. If the root is set apart for service to God, so are the branches.

17) And if some of the branches were broken off, and you Gentiles, like a wild olive tree, were grafted in among them, **18)** do not boast that you are superior to the natural branches which were broken off.

When you boast, you forget that you did not bring life to the root, but the root brought life to you.

19) Perhaps you Gentiles will say, "The natural branches were broken off so I might be grafted in."

20) It is true that they were broken off, but not for that reason. They were broken off because of their unbelief, and you can only continue by faith. Do not be proud, but humble.

21) For if God did not spare the natural branches, be careful lest He spare you not. **22)** But rather consider God's goodness and His sternness—on those who fell, you see His sternness—in your own case you see His goodness.

23) If the natural branches do not continue in unbelief, they shall be grafted in again for God is at liberty to graft them in again when their unbelief is gone. This is not at all impossible. **24)** For if you were cut out of the wild olive tree, and were grafted into the good olive tree, an unnatural process; how much more feasible is it that these natural olive branches should be grafted into their own olive tree.

25) I say these things because I do not want you to be ignorant of this hitherto unknown fact, lest you should be wise in your own conceits, that this judicial hardening has come upon part of Israel only until the time of the fulness of the Gentiles. 26) Then all believing Israel shall be saved, as it is written, "Then shall come a Savior for Zion's sake and He shall turn away ungodliness from Jacob. 27) For this is My agreement with them at the time when I shall remove their sins."

28) As far as the Gospel is concerned, they are being treated as enemies so that you might be blessed. But as far as God's election is concerned, they are still beloved for the fathers' sake.

29) For the gifts and choices of God are not subject to reconsideration or change of mind.

30) In former times you did not believe God, yet you have obtained mercy from God because of their unbelief. 31) In the same way, they do not believe now, but the result will be that through your conversion, they will be provoked to jealousy and will be converted. 32) For God has delivered all men to a condition of unbelief so that He can have mercy on all of them.

33) O the depths of the riches both of the wisdom and knowledge of God. How unsearchable are His decisions, and His methods beyond our knowledge! 34) For who has ever known the mind of the Lord, or who has counselled Him? 35) Or who has ever placed God under obligation by giving anything to Him? 36) No one has, because God is self-contained—of Him and through Him and to Him are all things—to Him be glory for ever. Amen.

GROUP DISCUSSION QUESTIONS
Chapter 9 — The Case of the Jew

1. How does Paul show us that we can become a descendant or "child of the Promise" which God made to Abraham?

2. Look at Romans 9:30-33. Do people still try to get to heaven by following laws? What does God say is the only real way to heaven?

3. Why is it important to "confess with your mouth" (Romans 10:9-19) what you believe in your heart? How many ways can you think of to do this?

4. Did God harden the hearts of the Israelites before or after they had chosen to go their own way instead of God's? Can they ever come back to Him for salvation? Can a person who has sinned a great deal repent and be redeemed?

Chapter Ten

Love Fulfills the Law

Romans 12-13

We now come to what is known as the practical portion of the epistle. The earlier chapters have revealed what God has done for us. Now we learn how we should respond to Him by lives of devotion and service.

HOW SHOULD CHRISTIANS BEHAVE?

There are numerous obligations which rest on those who have been saved by grace.

Consecration to God is the first of these (vv. 1, 2). These are certainly among the most important verses in the epistle, and it would be a tragedy to finish the course and yet miss their message. As Paul considers all that God has done, as revealed in the previous chapters, he feels impelled to make a very strong appeal to his readers, "Present your bodies a living sacrifice, holy, acceptable unto God."

The mercies of God to the sinner saved by grace leave him with only one reasonable conclusion, "If God has done all this for me, then I must give my body to Him. If Christ died for me, the least I can do is to live for Him."

> "O Christ, Thy bleeding hands and feet,
>   Thy sacrifice for me;
>   Each wound, each tear demands my life
>   A sacrifice for Thee."

It was C. T. Studd who said, "If Jesus Christ is God and died for me, then no sacrifice can be too great for me to make for Him."

And Isaac Watts wrote the now-familiar lines:

"Were the whole realm of nature mine,
That were an offering far too small;
Love so amazing, so divine,
Demands my heart, my life, my all."

These words are true. In fact, one of the greatest contradictions in the universe is a Christian who lives to please himself rather than the Lord who bought him. Our lives should be yielded to Him moment by moment so that He can use us in whatever way He pleases.

Then, secondly, Paul urges his readers not to be conformed to the world. We should be different. Instead of thinking like the world does, we should look at things as God sees them. After all, it was the world that crucified our Savior, and so we should be separated from it in all our thoughts and ways.

As we thus yield our bodies to God, and renew our minds by thinking His thoughts, we will come to know what His good and acceptable and perfect will is for us, and then our lives will really count for eternity.

Humility in the exercise of gifts is another obligation (vv. 3-8). Everything we have was given to us from above. Therefore, we should not be proud of any special abilities we may have, but should simply seek to use them for His glory.

Love to the saints is demanded of believers (vv. 9-13). Our love should be sincere, pure, unselfish and kind.

Love to one's persecutors is expected of us (vv. 14-21). The Christian should not seek revenge, but leave the matter of judgment to the Lord. The best policy is to repay persecution with kindness.

Subjection to the government is mandatory for Christians (13:1-7). Since the civil powers are ordained of God, the child of God should be obedient, not just for fear of punishment, but for conscience sake. Of course, the saint's first loyalty is to God, and he should not let any government compel him to do anything that would be contrary to the

Word of God. However, in matters of paying taxes and customs, the believer has definite obligations to the higher powers.

Love to one's neighbors is a Christian obligation (vv. 8-10). This is a debt we owe to all men.

> "Let me look on the crowd as my Savior did,
> Till my eyes with tears grow dim.
> Let me view with pity the wandering sheep,
> And love them for love of Him."

Watchful waiting for the Lord's return marks out the believer (vv. 11-14). Everything we do should be judged by the possibility of His coming. The twofold secret of Christian living is to (1) put on the Lord Jesus Christ, that is, be so occupied with Him and so anxious to please Him that others will see Him in you; (2) make no provision for the flesh. Refuse its promptings and passions. Do not cater to it or trifle with it.

REVIEW
Paraphrase of Romans 12-13

Chapter 12

1) I urge you, therefore, brethren, in view of all God's kindness to you, that you present your bodies a living sacrifice, without blemish, well-pleasing unto God, which is your reasonable service.

2) And do not be molded according to the pattern of this wicked world, but be transformed by an entirely new attitude of mind, so that you may prove the good, acceptable and perfect will of God in your own lives.

3) For I say, through the favor that has been shown to me, to every one among you, that you should not have an exaggerated idea of your own importance. But you should think sensibly, taking into consideration the particular abilities which God has given to you. **4)** For just as we have many members in one body, and these members do not have the same function, **5)** so we Christians, a great host, are one body in Christ, and we are members of one another. **6)** Seeing then that our abilities are different, depending on God's gracious dealings with us, let us each perform his function well. If our gift is to be a spokesman for God, let us do so to the extent that He has enabled us. **7)** Or if our gift is to minister to others, let us attend to our ministering. Or if it is to teach, let us teach faithfully. **8)** Or if it is to exhort, let us devote ourselves to exhorting. The one whose gift is to give for the support of others, let him do so with liberality. The one whose gift is to be a leader, let him do it diligently. And the one whose function it is to sympathize with others, let him do so cheerfully.

9) Let your love be sincere. Despise that which is evil; cling to that which is good. **10)** Be kindly affectioned toward one another, showing the same love you would to your own brother. In all honorable acts, set an example to others; **11)** not slothful in your activities, but fervent in spirit; serving the Lord; **12)** rejoicing in the hope set before you; patient in tribulation; continuing fervently in prayer; **13)** providing for the needs of the saints; given to hospitality.

14) Bless those who persecute you; bless, and do not curse them. **15)** Rejoice with those who rejoice, and weep with those who weep. **16)** Be kindly disposed toward one another. Do not chase after high things, but associate with lowly men. Do not be proud in your own conceits. **17)** Do not repay with evil when you are wronged; but act in a way that will commend you to all men. **18)** Insofar as you are able to do so, live at peace with all men. **19)** Dearly beloved, do not seek revenge, but rather leave the matter to be taken care of by God's wrath, for it is written, "Vengeance belongs to me; I will repay, saith the Lord." **20)** Thus if your enemy is hungry, feed him. If he is thirsty, give him water to drink. For in doing this, you will heap coals of fire on his head, that is, you will subdue him with kindness. **21)** Do not let evil get the best of you, but overcome evil with good.

Chapter 13

1) Let every individual be obedient to governmental authorities. For there is no government independent of God. The existing governments are ordained of God. **2)** Whoever therefore resists the government resists that which God has decreed. And those who resist shall be punished.

3) Again, rulers do not terrorize those who do good, but only those who do evil. Do you wish to be free from fear of the government? Then obey the ruler and he will commend you. **4)** For he is a servant of God, appointed to promote your welfare. But if you do that which is evil, then you might well fear; for it is not in vain that he has the authority to punish; for he is a servant of God, a revenger to punish the evil-doer.

5) And so you must be obedient, not only because of fear of punishment, but also so that you can have a clear conscience toward God.

6) For these same considerations, you should pay taxes also. For rulers are God's servants, devoting their time continually to the affairs of government. **7)** Give therefore to every man what rightly belongs to him; taxes to whom taxes are due; custom to whom custom; reverence to whom reverence; respect to whom respect.

8) Pay all your debts, especially this one—that of loving one another. This one is always outstanding. **9)** For the following commandments:

Thou shalt not commit adultery

Thou shalt not kill

Thou shalt not steal

Thou shalt not bear false witness

Thou shalt not covet

and any other commandments are all included in this one:

Thou shalt love thy neighbor as thyself.

10) Love never causes any wrong to be done to a man's neighbor. Therefore love is the fulfillment of the law.

11) And that is all the more imperative when we consider the times in which we live; that now it is high time to awake out of sleep; for our complete salvation, the salvation of our bodies as well as our souls, is nearer now than when we believed. **12)** The night is almost gone; the day is near; let us renounce those things which are done in darkness and let us don the armor of light. **13)** Let us live decently, as in the day time; not in carousing and drunkenness, nor in immorality and lust, nor in strife and envying.

14) But display the life of the Lord Jesus Christ, and do not cater to the flesh, or to gratifying its evil desires.

GROUP DISCUSSION QUESTIONS
Chapter 10 — Love Fullfils the Law

1. How can a christian be a living sacrifice (Romans 12:1)?

2. What are the important contributions to the Body of Christ that you have seen in others? What contribution can you make?

3. In Romans 12:9-21 Paul gives many practical ways in which we can show love to each other, discuss these ways.

4. Do any of these ways of showing love say that you must "feel loving" before you do them? What does this mean for the person who wants to follow Jesus? Or what practical implications does this have?

5. What does Romans 13 say about cheating on taxes?

6. What simple guideline do we learn from Romans 13:8-10? In what areas of life can we use this rule? How could this guideline change someone's behavior?

Chapter Eleven

The Weak Brother

Romans 14:1—15:13

Paul has been showing how a Christian should conduct himself in various relationships both within and without the sphere of Christian fellowship. Now he deals with a most practical issue indeed—

HOW SHOULD CHRISTIANS BEHAVE ONE TOWARDS ANOTHER?

Tolerance to the brother who is weak (14—15:13) is an important rule of Christian conduct. The Apostle here begins a discussion of two types of Christians, the weak and the strong. The weak brother is one who feels he cannot, as a believer, eat certain types of food, or who feels he must observe certain religious days. Perhaps this type of person was originally of Jewish background, and continued to hold some of these beliefs after his conversion.

The strong brother is one who realizes that these matters are of no importance to God. The Christian is at liberty to eat all kinds of wholesome foods, and is not bound to the observance of a church calendar.

Realizing that the presence of these two types of individuals might cause conflict in the church, Paul now urges a spirit of loving tolerance. First, he addresses them individually, then unitedly. (It should be noted that the principles set down here only apply to inconsequential matters, such as food and drink. They must not be applied to doctrines or duties which are clearly taught in the Bible.)

To the strong Paul says, You should receive the weak brother into your fellowship, and not for the purpose of starting a controversy with him (v. 1). You should not despise the weak brother (v. 3a). To the weak he says, Do not condemn the strong brother (v. 3b). After all, God has received him (v. 3b). He is God's servant and accountable to God (v. 4). You may think he will fall into sin because of his attitude, but God will keep him from falling (v. 4).

To both the strong and weak Paul says, and notice the following series of "lets"—Let every man be fully persuaded in his own mind about these matters of moral indifference. Christ is our Lord and we must do all with a view to pleasing Him (vv. 5-9). Let us not judge others. We will have to give an account of ourselves, not of others, at the Judgment Seat of Christ (vv. 10-13a). Let us not be a cause of offense to others (vv. 13b-15). Things that are harmless to some are sinful to others. We are wrong if we grieve others over such matters. It does not show true love for them. To tempt them to sin is to wreck those for whom Christ died. They might become discouraged and cease to make progress in the Christian life, for instance. Let not your good be evil spoken of (vv. 16-18). The things that really count are not material, such as food and drink, but spiritual. Those who recognize this distinction are approved by God. Let us adopt this twofold standard—does it make for peace, and does it edify (vv. 19-23)?

If we follow this rule we will not let inconsequential things wreck the work God is doing in another believer's life. We will do nothing that would cause a brother to stumble, or be offended, or be made weak. We will not proudly parade our Christian liberty. We will not do what our conscience condemns.

Let us live to please others rather than ourselves (15:2-6). The Savior did not please Himself. Certainly we should follow His example. Therefore, let us receive one another (15:7-13). Christ has received both Jew and Gentile. We should receive both weak and strong.

REVIEW
Paraphrase of Romans 14:1—15:13

Chapter 14

1) Receive into your fellowship the man who is weak in the Christian faith, but do not be a judge of his opinions. 2) For one man believes that he may eat everything; another, who is weak, eats only vegetables. 3) Do not let the one who eats a certain thing look down on the one who does not. And do not let him who does not eat it criticize the one who does, because God has accepted him. 4) Who authorized you to criticize another man's servant? It is to his own master that he is accountable. And do not think that he will fall into sin, because God will hold him up. 5) One man feels that a certain day is more sacred than another day; some other man believes that all days are of equal importance. Let every man be fully convinced on these matters in his own mind. 6) The one who values one day above another does it out of respect to the Lord. The one who does not differentiate between days is seeking to honor the Lord, too. The one who feels free to eat all types of food, is seeking to please the Lord, for he thanks God for it. The one who does not eat all foods is likewise striving to be pleasing to the Lord, and he gives thanks for his food, too.

7) For none of us lives for his own pleasure, neither do we die for our own convenience. 8) Thus while we live, we live for the Lord's glory, and when we die, it is for the Lord's glory, too. Whether we live or die, we are the Lord's. 9) For that is why Christ both died and lived again, namely, that He might become Lord of the dead and the living.

10) So why should you pass judgment on your brother? Or why should you belittle your brother? For we shall all stand before the judgment seat of Christ. 11) Just as it is written, "As I live, saith the Lord, every knee shall bow to Me and every tongue shall confess to God." 12) So then every one of us shall give account of himself to God. 13) Therefore, let us not criticize one another any more, but rather let us determine that no one puts a stumbling-block or a cause of failure in the way of a brother.

14) I know, and am fully persuaded by the teachings of the Lord Jesus, that no food is in itself unclean. But if a man considers a certain food to be unclean, then it is unclean to him. 15) And so, if your brother is offended by seeing you eating meat, then you are not walking in a kindly manner. Do not offend by your food one for whom Christ died. 16) Do not let that which is legitimate for you be made the subject of evil reports. 17) For the important things in God's kingdom are not foods and drinks, but the righteousness, joy

and peace which are given by the Holy Spirit. **18)** And the man who displays these virtues in his service for Christ finds favor with God, and approval with men.

19) Let us therefore try to promote peace among us, and endeavor to edify one another. **20)** Do not, for your appetite for certain foods, pull down what God is building up. It is indeed true that all things are pure, but it is wrong for any man to use them as a cause of offense. **21)** It is a good rule neither to eat meat nor to drink wine, nor to take anything which stumbles your brother or offends him, or by which he is weakened in the faith.

22) Do you have faith that all things are lawful for you? Well, hold on to that belief in private before God. Happy is the man who has a clear conscience to do the things that he believes are right. **23)** On the other hand, the one who has doubts concerning the lawfulness of certain foods is condemned when he eats them, because he is not eating with the assurance that he is right, for whatever is not done in the confidence that it is right is wrong.

Chapter 15

1) So then those of us who are strong in faith should tolerate the views held by our weak brethren, and should not seek to please ourselves. **2)** Rather, let each of us seek to please his neighbor so he might be benefited by being edified.

3) For even Christ pleased not Himself, but He lived to please God, as it is written, "The insults of those who insulted Thee were felt by Me."

4) Now all the divine literature of the past was written for our instruction so that we might be sustained by hope, through the patience and consolation which come to us through the Scriptures.

5) Now may the God who alone is the source of patience and consolation grant you to be like-minded toward one another according to the example of Jesus Christ, **6)** so that you may with one mind and one mouth glorify the God and Father of our Lord Jesus Christ. **7)** Thus receive one another as Christ received you (Gentiles) to the glory of God. **8)** Now I want to emphasize this that Christ received you Gentiles in order that you might glorify God. Jesus Christ was, first of all, a minister to the Jews. His office was to maintain the truth of God by fulfilling the promise made to the Jewish patriarchs.

9) But He also came in order that the Gentiles might glorify God for the mercy He showed to them. This is stated in the following Old Testament Scriptures. David said, "For this cause I will confess to Thee among the Gentiles, and sing unto Thy Name." **10)** And it is also written, "Rejoice, ye

Gentiles, with His people." **11)** And again, "Praise the Lord, all ye Gentiles; and laud Him, all ye people." **12)** And then Isaiah said, "There shall be a root of Jesse, and He that shall rise to reign over the Gentiles; in Him shall the Gentiles hope."

13) Now then, may the God of hope fill you with all joy and peace as you trust in Him so that you may abound in hope through the power of the Holy Spirit.

GROUP DISCUSSION QUESTIONS
Chapter 11 — The Weak Brother

1. What kinds of rules do people impose on themselves and others which are not given in the Bible?

2. Discuss Romans 14:14. Is it necessary for each person to do or to avoid doing the same things in order for them to have the same faith in Jesus?

3. How are we to act when we are with someone who believes differently than we do about something? Why? (Romans 14:12-22)

4. Does Romans 15:1-13 explain why there are different Christian Churches? What should the attitude and actions of these different groups of believers be towards each other?

Chapter Twelve

People and Places

Romans 15:14—16:27

The time has come for Paul to conclude his epistle. He has discussed the need for the Gospel, its nature and its implications. He concludes with a brief discussion of his plans and with personal greetings.

PAUL'S PLANS

First of all, Paul gives his reasons for writing the letter (vv. 14-21). He wanted to remind them of these great truths so that his work as apostle to the Gentiles might be acceptable to God.

Next, Paul discusses his plans for the immediate future (vv. 22-33). He hopes to visit Rome on his trip to Spain. In the meantime, however, he is going to Jerusalem with a gift of money for the poor saints there from the Christians in Macedonia and Achaia. In view of his plans, he asks them to pray for the success of his mission in Jerusalem, for deliverance from unbelievers, and for blessing on his ministry when he reaches Rome.

PERSONAL GREETINGS

Personal greetings to the saints (chapter 16). At first glance the closing chapter of Romans seems to be an uninteresting catalog of names that have little or no meaning to us today. However, upon closer study, this neglected chapter yields many precious lessons for the believer.

The Christians listed here are living examples of the truths taught in the epistle. How fitting it is to close the letter with a picture of truth in action. Paul shows a deep personal interest in and love for the saints. He was pleased by news of their progress and proud of their steadfast devotion to Christ. We should maintain the same attitude toward our fellow-believers.

Some Bible students have made the interesting suggestion that Romans 16 is a miniature of the Judgment Seat of Christ. There is praise for every instance of faithfulness to the Lord.

The entire chapter is a commentary on Christian greatness. These people were not famous as far as the world was concerned, but their names are enshrined forever in God's Word.

Personal names often have meanings which are interesting and instructive. For instance, Epaenetus means "praiseworthy," and Philologus means "lover of the word." No doubt, these men lived up to their names.

Letter writing is a great ministry. We never know how God will use what we write, when we write for His glory and for the help and encouragement of His people. God rewards every kindness done in His Name. This section shows that little deeds of kindness are noticed and recorded by Him.

The chapter shows that letters of commendation were carried by Christians going from one church or assembly to another (v. 1). This is a means of excluding unbelievers and imposters from the fellowship of the local church. The prominence of women's names in this chapter emphasizes their wide sphere of usefulness (vv. 1, 3, 6, 7, etc.). Public preaching is not the only work that counts for God.

This closing section is an outstanding example of Christian courtesy. It is obviously the work of a gentleman. The chapter evidences a lack of officialism and class distinctions among the saints. They were "all one in Christ Jesus." It is apparent that there was a very close fellowship among the believers. It would seem that Christianity was the absorbing passion of their lives, and that this common interest bound them together. The simplicity of the New Testament church is suggested. As we read in verse 5, "the church that is in their house," we can picture a group of saints meeting in a home for worship, prayer and fellowship.

In verses 17-19, we have a warning against those who cause divisions. It is a warning, incidentally, that is still needed today.

Finally, we learn that hospitality must be very important in God's estimation, because it is mentioned often and commended always.

And now at the conclusion of our study of this wonderful epistle, we would say with Paul, "The grace of our Lord Jesus Christ be with you all! Amen."

REVIEW
Paraphrase of Romans 15:14—16:27

Chapter 15

14) Indeed, as I have written these exhortations to you, I have been fully conscious of your state, brethren, that you are full of kindness, well-taught, and able to instruct one another. **15)** In spite of this, I have written to you more bluntly, in some ways, than would seem necessary in order to remind you of these things, because that is the gracious task that God has entrusted to me, **16)** namely, that I should be the minister of Jesus Christ to the Gentiles, acting as a priest with respect to the Gospel of God so that the Gentiles, as a sacrifice, might be acceptable to God, being sanctified by the Holy Spirit.

17) In view of this special mission, I have legitimate reason for boasting through Jesus Christ in divine matters. **18)** In doing so, I would not venture to mention any successes which Christ has not brought about directly through me. He has used me to make the Gentiles obedient to the Gospel in word and deed, **19)** using mighty signs and wonders in the power of the Spirit of God. The result of His blessing is that I have fully preached the Gospel of Christ in the area from Jerusalem to all around Illyricum. **20)** Yes, I have tried to preach the Gospel where Christ was not known, lest I should reap the results of another man's work. **21)** As it is written, "To whom He was not spoken of, they shall see; and they that have not heard shall understand." **22)** It is for this reason that I have been prevented for a long time from visiting you.

23) But now, inasmuch as my work is finished in these areas, and because I have had a great desire for many years to visit you, **24)** whenever I make my trip to Spain, I will visit you, for I hope to see you on my trip, and to be sped onward to Spain by you, after I have finished my stay with you.

25) But now I am going to Jerusalem to distribute funds to the saints. **26)** For the Christians of Macedonia and Achaia have seen fit to make a donation to poor saints in Jerusalem. **27)** They have desired to do this, and well indeed they might. For if the Gentiles have shared their spiritual blessings, then their duty is to share their material resources with the Jews.

28) Whenever, then, I have done this, and handed over to them this deserved reward, I will visit you en route to Spain. **29)** And I am confident that when I do visit you, I shall be accompanied by the abundant blessings of the Gospel of Christ.

30) Now I earnestly urge, brethren, for the sake of the Lord Jesus Christ, and for the love of the Spirit, that you join with me in true prayer to God on my behalf **31)** that I may be delivered from the unbelievers in Judea, that my mission in Jerusalem might be successful, **32)** and that I may come to you with joy, Lord willing, and may be refreshed with you.

Chapter 16

1) I commend to your fellowship our sister Phebe, who is a servant of the church at Cenchrea, **2)** asking that you receive her in the Lord, as saints should do, and that you assist her in any matters in which she needs your help. For she has been a benefactor of many, including myself.

3) Salute Priscilla and Aquila, my co-laborers in Christ Jesus, **4)** who have risked their own lives for my safety. Not only I, but all the Gentile churches are thankful to them.

5) Likewise, salute the church that meets in their house.

Salute my well-beloved Epanetus, who is the first convert in Asia to Christ.

6) Salute Mary, who worked hard for me. **7)** Salute Andronicus and Junia, my relatives and my fellow prisoners who are well known among the apostles, and who were Christians before me.

8) Salute Amplias, my beloved in the Lord.

9) Salute Urbane, our helper in Christ, and Stachys, my beloved.

10) Salute Apelles, approved in Christ.

Salute those in Aristobulus' household.

11) Salute Herodion, my relative. Salute those of Narcissus' household who are Christians. **12)** Salute Tryphena and Tryphosa who are busy for the Lord. Salute Persis who has been a diligent worker for the Lord. **13)** Salute Rufus, a choice Christian, and his mother and mine.

14) Salute Asyncritus, Phlegon, Hermas, Patrobas, Hermes, and the brethren who are with them. **15)** Salute Philologus, and Julia, Nereus and his sister, and Olympas and all the saints who are with them.

16) Salute one another with a holy kiss.

17) Now I urge you, brethren, to note carefully those who cause divisions, and do things contrary to the teaching which you have learned, and avoid them. **18)** For such men do not serve the Lord Jesus, but rather their own appetites. By enticing words and pleasant speech, they deceive the minds of the unwary ones.

19) It is true that your obedience is well known, and I am thankful for it, but yet I should like you to be wise to do good, and simple to avoid evil.

20) And the God of peace shall bruise Satan under your feet shortly. The grace of our Lord Jesus Christ be with you, Amen.

21) Timothy, my fellow worker, salutes you; also Lucius, Jason, and Sosipater, my relatives.

22) I, Tertius, who did the writing of this letter salute you in the Lord.

23) Gaius, my host, and not only my host, but the host of all the Christians, salutes you; also Erastus, the city treasurer, and Quartus, a brother.

24) The grace of our Lord Jesus Christ be with you all. Amen.

25) Now to God who is able to thoroughly establish you with reference to my Gospel, with reference to the teachings of Jesus Christ, and with reference to the revelation of that mystery (Christ and the Church) which has been kept secret since the world began, **26)** but now is made manifest, and by the prophetic Scriptures, by edict of the everlasting God is made known to all nations that they should receive it by faith,—**27)** to God only wise, be glory through Jesus Christ for ever. Amen.

GROUP DISCUSSION QUESTIONS
Chapter 12 — People and Places

1. In Romans 16:1-15 Paul is commending different people from the church of that day. Do you know people who could be praised for having these same characteristics?

2. In Romans 16:17-20 Paul gives a warning. Restate this in your own words. How can each person avoid the danger Paul warns against?

3. Notice that approximately an equal number of men and women are mentioned specifically by Paul in these final greetings. What does this show us in regard to his respect for women?

4. To better understand the "mystery" which Paul describes in the final prayer of Romans 16:25-27, read I Corinthians 2 aloud. What does verse 26 tell us is God's reason for revealing this mystery now?

MY
PERSONAL ANSWER

In the spaces below, an opportunity is given for every student to state exactly where he stands with regard to his soul's salvation.

Please check in the appropriate space and return with your last lesson.

However, before completing this form, you should solemnly consider the inescapable fact that you will be banished from God for all eternity if you reject His Son (Hebrews 2:3).

Please check one only:

☐ Before enrolling in this course, I had been born again by receiving Christ as my personal Savior.

☐ During the study of these lessons, I have received the Lord Jesus Christ by faith.

☐ I here and now receive the Lord Jesus as my Savior.

☐ I am definitely interested in being saved, but I should like to have additional information regarding the following subjects:

_____

_____

_____

_____

_____

☐ I am still not saved.

_____

(Your name)

PLEASE MAIL THIS SHEET WITH LAST EXAM